MW01050076

A STRESS-FREE FAMILY
Chaos to Calm in Only 28 Days

Madeleine Davis

Copyright © Madeleine Davis, 2018. All Rights Reserved.

No part of this publication may be reproduced, stored in a retrieval system, or transmitted in any form or by any means, electronic, mechanical, photocopy, recording or otherwise, without prior written permission of the copyright owner. Nor can it be circulated in any form of binding or cover other than that in which it is published and without similar condition including this condition being imposed on a subsequent purchaser.

Any queries relating to this publication or author may be sent to mdavis@theparentingsystem.com

I'm grateful you've gotten my book!
I'd like to offer you my e-guide as a

FREE GIFT
"How to Stop Nagging Your Kids"

This short e-guide will provide you with a fast and stress-free way to stop nagging your kids;

It's yours… **FREE to download at:**
http://thestressfreefamily.com/go

Table of Contents

THE FIVE PILLARS OF THE 28-DAY STRESS-FREE FAMILY SYSTEM ARE:

> Routines
> Rhythms
> Rules
> Rewards
> Revolutionize

We'll be covering all 5 Pillars on the following days:

Dedication

This book and everything else is dedicated to the 4 loves of my life. My husband, Eric, and my 3 sons, Zachary, Max, and Carson. You are my every breath. Every day is filled with awe and love for you. Thank you for making me want to do better and to be better and for being YOU. I am grateful every moment for US.

Acknowledgment and Gratitude

To my parents Leon and Marta and my siblings Anna, Lenora, and Marc: Family is everything. I'm thankful always for your love and support. I'd especially like to acknowledge my sister and role model, Anna. Some moms are born with it, some aren't. She was, and I wasn't. Without judgement, she inspired my transformation and allowed me to see what was possible.

Thank you to my in-laws, Ira and Eleanor and Alicia. When I fell in love with Eric, you were an amazing bonus. Thank you for taking me into your beautiful family.

I'm grateful for Priscilla, Gordon, my brother-in-laws, Michael and Stephen and my nieces and nephews, Steven, Julia, Sam, Aaron, Ethan, Jessie.

I also want to send a huge 'Thank you' to my extended family and friends. We know it takes a village to raise a child, but it also takes a village to support a mother. I'm grateful for my village.

Thank you to the head of my brand agency, Doug Crowe, who believed in my message and my mission and guaranteed my success. Your support, direction, and encouragement has been invaluable.

Thank you to my editor, Melissa Lehman. Knowing that I could hand you my manuscript and that you'd get my message and my voice across clearly helped me bring *The 28-Day Stress-Free Family System* to life in a stress-free way!

My passion is helping overwhelmed moms create high-functioning, stress-free homes so they can relax, *knowing* they are giving their kids a strong foundation. Homes where Moms are unshakably confident they're setting their kids up for success. I believe that the mother is the head and the heart of the home. So, when I affect one mom, it ripples out into the universe, as she affects everyone she touches. Thank you to the past and future moms I have the honor to work with. And thank YOU for reading this book, starting your journey to a Stress-Free Family, and allowing me to spread my mission and my message.

Introduction:
Don't skip this. Start Here!

Hello! I can't tell you how happy I am that you are beginning your journey with *The 28-Day Stress-Free Family System. This is going to transform your family in so many ways*. I'm also excited for you because I am confident that, in no time at all, you will go from *learning about* my 28-day plan, to *committing to* my 28-day plan to transform your home into one that's calm, relaxed, stress-free, and high-functioning. I know you're going to commit because the plan *works*. My children and I, and all the moms I've worked with have become stress-free using this system – we are living proof.

During the 28-day plan, you are going to learn how and why the five Pillars of my system – Routines, Rhythms, Rules, and Rewards – will Revolutionize your home. It sounds too good to be true, doesn't it? But it's not! Not if you stick to the plan. Follow the system, and the stress in your home will be all but gone because:

- Your children will:
  - Learn to listen and respond respectfully – in ways that result in desired behaviors.
  - Know what to do and when to do it.
  - Know what to expect from you and what is expected of them.
  - Understand what Rewards and consequences are in store for them, based on their behavior.
  - Learn to effectively and respectfully communicate with you.

- You will:
    o Learn how to create and carry out Routines that are reasonable, functional, and tailored to your family's needs. This will allow your family to "get in the flow."
    o Learn to make and adhere to Rules based on your family's values and principles, as well as how to effectively communicate and enforce those Rules.
    o Learn to develop reasonable expectations and communicate them to your children to evoke positive responses, actions, and behaviors.
    o Learn to communicate in a firm but loving manner that is effective, efficient, and produces the desired results.

Who doesn't want a household like that, right? I'd like to take a few moments to spell out how this system is different than other parenting programs and to share a little about myself and my journey in creating my own Stress-Free Family.

How Is This System Different?

There are several things about *The 28-Day Stress-Free Family System* that may sound familiar from other parenting plans. First, many plans for streamlining your household involve helping your children develop Routines, such as one to prepare for the next morning before bedtime. Other plans focus on choosing the right words to elicit desired behavior or letting children experience the consequences of their actions. My plan includes these elements, but with a few tweaks and twists that I'll call my *Signature Moves*. These *Signature Moves* are very simple details, but they make this system *profoundly* different from other parenting programs. Plus, I have some *Signature Moves* that you will not find in *any* other parenting system!

Next, The 28-Day Stress-Free Family System *integrates* all the elements you'll find in other parenting programs – plus a few more. Instead of trying to fix just one thing, we take a holistic approach by addressing the whole family and its dynamic. This simple shift in perspective creates significantly better results!

Finally, it works better than other systems because of how we introduce the changes to your kids. I teach you how to do the system without telling your children! Why? By keeping things under wraps, we avoid dealing with kids' pushback or anxiety about changes and new expectations. The last thing you want to do is institute "another thing" without maximizing your chances for success. Keeping it quiet – *for now* – allows you to practice getting it right and to experience success. Too many times, we try "another thing" and give up before we can get it to take hold. Then your family tends to expect that from you, and you feel even more defeated.

We also want your kids to practice and experience success with the system and to enjoy the benefits, such as a calmer home, less anxiety, being on time, etc. before we tell them that there is a system. Plus, when we get to the last Pillar, "Revolutionize," they find out how they'll be rewarded for implementing the system. And, since they've already been practicing, they will already know how to do it! EASY Rewards – for both them and you! Trust me when I tell you that 'stealth mode' works best for implementing this system!

Who Am I, and How Do I Know This Will Work for You and Your Family?

That's right! I haven't formally introduced myself. I'm Madeleine Davis, a mom to three amazing children who got a wake-up call one morning. That 'call' made me painfully aware that something had to change because our life was pure chaos. And by the end of that day, I realized that the 'something' that needed to change was me.

I'm going to tell that story – in all its embarrassing detail – in just a minute. But first, let me explain how I know The 28-Day Stress-Free Family System is going to transform your family!

- I am a "Before" and "After" case study. I didn't create this program because I was BORN a "together mom." I was a "disaster" mom. I know what our life was like before I created my system, and I know how completely different it is now. My "Before" and "After" are night and day, so I know the plan brings the desired results and makes life better for EVERYONE in the home.

- I've helped moms, just like you, transform their families from chaotic to calm using this 28-day system – it works!

- I see kids and parents flailing around like fish out of water, wanting to 'do family' better but not knowing how or where to start. As a result, they are living in the state of chaos my family used to live in. I know what it did to me and to my children, so I know what it is doing to your children and to *you*. And it breaks my heart. Parents and children deserve more than chaos. They deserve a calm, loving home, flowing with positive energy.

Okay, now I'll tell you how this stress-free system was born from one super-embarrassing morning and one "light bulb" conversation. Can you feel me blushing through these words? Here it goes.

It was a typical morning in our house – yelling, nagging, and scurrying around like chickens without their heads. Despite the chaos and scrambling, we managed to get out of the house on time – a little early, even. So, after walking my two older kids to their respective schools (welcome to NYC!), my youngest and I arrived at preschool, a few minutes early.

I thought, "What? Is this for real? Could I become one of the 'early moms' and have time to sit on benches outside the school instead of rushing past them to get my child into school and *trying* not be late for work?"

I must admit, I was feeling pretty darn proud of myself – smug, even. Even though I had just spent the last hour yelling at my kids to get ready, nagging at them to hurry up, and I'd left my home looking like a bomb had gone off inside. None of that mattered at that shining moment, because we made it to school early! I felt like maybe I was getting better at this juggling act. I mean, I was there, sitting on the same bench with the "early moms," right?

Then something unexpected happened. A mom sitting across from me asked me how I managed to get three kids to three schools on time *and* 'keep it all together'. I thought, "Who ME? Why does she think I have it all together?" I'd spent the morning yelling at my kids to get ready, barely getting them fed, and left my home in complete shambles. But of course, she didn't know that.

Did she think I had it all together because I wasn't in sweats? I had thrown on a maxi dress only because it was the fastest thing I could throw on since I didn't have to think about a top and a bottom.

A part of me felt like a complete fraud, but part of me thought maybe, somehow, I COULD be one of "those" moms. A together mom. The mom who gets her kids to school early. The mom who looks put together. A mom whose home runs smoothly, effortlessly, and without stress.

While I sat there fantasizing about what it would be like to be a "together mom" and giving myself a few kudos for at least appearing to be one, I crossed my legs. And that's when it happened.

When I looked down, I was horrified to realize I was wearing two different shoes.

Yep, two…different…shoes.

Talk about bursting my bubble! While I was thinking I was on my way to becoming a "together mom," the reality was that I'd left my home, walked my kids to three different schools, and was at pre-school chatting with a bunch of other moms, all without even being aware that I was wearing two different shoes!

The walk home was what I call *my* (mom) walk of shame. Every single step I took was an in-my-face reminder that I was incompetent. I felt hopeless and overwhelmed. Why was this so hard for me? What was wrong with me? I was smart when it came to business, but at home, I couldn't get my kids to do anything without yelling and nagging. At home I felt inept and stupid. I also felt sad…for me and for my children.

That night, I called my sister, literally crying about my mom fails. My sister happens to be one of the lucky moms who was born with the "together mom" gene. She parents with ease - it all just came so naturally to her. Why did she get that gene and not me? It just wasn't fair. She said something that night that changed everything. She told me that although I didn't inherit the "together mom" gene, I was born with the "CEO gene." She helped me to see the parallels between running my businesses and running a home – and to start owning the fact that, as the mom, I am the CEO of my home. Wow! It was a huge 'eureka moment' for me. That conversation turned my feelings of hopelessness into a sense of empowerment and determination.

When we hung up, I began thinking about ways I could run my home like I ran my businesses – with policies, procedures, expectations and, incentives – *and* how I could effectively communicate these things to my kids. Suddenly, things started to make sense, and I knew I was going to be able to become the mom I wanted to be and the mom my children deserved. I knew we were going to have the *home* we deserved.

The changes didn't happen overnight. In fact, I started the system by making one significant decision and built the rest of the system on that. What was that decision? *I decided to decide.*

I decided that night to decide what I would wear the next day. I picked out clothes – AND shoes! – to wear the next day. The next morning, I noticed how that one little change in my Routine made a huge difference. *(And* that I wouldn't be reprising my role as Ms. Miss-Matched Shoes – Whew!) That tiny Routine shift worked remarkably well for me, so I started creating Routines for my kids. And this brings me to the Five Pillars of *The 28-Day Stress-Free Family System.* Allow me to introduce them all.

THE FIVE PILLARS OF THE 28-DAY STRESS-FREE FAMILY SYSTEM:

1. **Routines**: A Routine is how, one person, does the same things, in the same way, at the same time, every day. This is where *The 28-Day Stress-Free Family System* starts. Why? Because Routines are the foundation of our day. Therefore, if your daily Routine flows smoothly, chances are good - most everything else will, too. Creating Routines for your children will make your life easy.

2. **Rhythms**: Rhythms are like Routines – in that they include what, how, and when things are done – but Rhythms refer to processes that involve at least two people, instead of one. It's kind of like a dance – you have steps and your child has steps. If you don't quite grasp what I might be referring to here, don't worry. I'll walk you through exactly how to create effective Rhythms – and it's going to change your life! Rhythms are my *Super Signature Move* – my secret sauce – and every mom's favorite part of the system! Routines make your life easy, but Rhythms will make it effortless!

3. **Rules**: I actually prefer the term "expectations," but everyone understands the concept of "Rules." (Plus, it gives us another "R" word to help make the Pillars easier to remember!) My *Signature Move* for Rules is having a "Rules trifecta" – Rules for *Mom*, kids, and the home. (Yes, Rules for YOU, Mama

Bear. Trust me, it's going to help you, and you're going to love it!) Another difference in my system is creating Rules tailored to your family, based on your household's core values.

4.   **Rewards:** You'd think that "Rewards" would be self-explanatory, but again, I have *Signature Moves* when it comes to Rewards that set them apart from traditional Rewards systems (that often end up being more like bribes!). In The 28-Day Stress-Free Family System, kids are rewarded for successful completion of their everyday Routines and Rhythms and following the Rules, plus they have the opportunity to earn additional Rewards for going above and beyond. And it works like magic.

5.   **Revolutionize:** Once you implement the first four Pillars, we put it all together to Revolutionize your home! You'll bring your kids in on it and go over all the Pillars of the system. I'm going to teach you how to run a family meeting where the whole system becomes THEIR idea!

Trust me when I tell you that you and your family members are going to be amazed at yourselves!

What to Expect Over the Next 28 Days:

The pages ahead will walk you through the 28 days and include assignments for you to implement The 28-Day Stress-Free Family System in your home. When you take it one day at a time, completing each day's assignment, four weeks from now, you will know the entire system, be putting it into action, and be noticing dramatic changes in your home.

However, if you are like me, and want to get things done, like, *yesterday*, feel free to do more than one day at a time. Just stick to them in order and don't skip any steps!

On the other hand, if you want to take longer, or if you experience obstacles along the way, and you need to take longer than 28 days, that is also *just fine*. I don't care if it takes you two weeks, 28 days, or *six months* to implement the system. I only ask that you do it in order, don't skip any steps and do what's best for you and your family. *Don't give up!* You deserve the stress-free results that you'll experience with this system. Stick with it for your family *and* for yourself!

Are you ready? I know I'm ready and excited to help you go from where you are now to where you want (and deserve) to be.

Today's Assignment:

Technically the 28 days begin on Day 1, so there's no formal assignment you need to complete before you continue with your reading. Therefore, your only "homework" is to get excited! Big changes are on the horizon for you and your family – and you deserve it!

Day 1:
Pillar 1 Routines – Ready…Set…Get Ready to Go

Today's Overview:

- *Signature Moves*
  - o Putting together an *integrated* system
  - o Keeping it a secret from the kids
  - o Deciding how, when, or even *if* your parenting partner will be involved
- What you'll need
  - o A dedicated journal for your assignments

"If nothing ever changed, there would be no butterflies."

~ Anonymous

Now *there's* a mom who knows how to do things right – Mother Nature! If she can change a squishy, fuzzy caterpillar into a beautiful butterfly, you can change your chaotic home into a calm one! Imagine you're the caterpillar, inching away at life right now, but you are about to take flight as a beautiful, butterfly, who's no longer "weighed down" by the stress in your home.

Before we get started on this transformation process, let me introduce you to the guidelines I recommend for success. These guidelines will allow you to implement the plan way it is supposed to – which is *easily and effortlessly.*

Think of today as the day we're wrapping ourselves in the chrysalis, preparing for our transformation into that amazing butterfly. Today, I have two simple assignments for you to prepare yourself. Then tomorrow, we'll get right into the system and begin our transformation!

The first thing you need to do to get ready to get ready is read and commit to the following:

THE 28-DAY STRESS-FREE FAMILY SYSTEM GUIDELINES

<u>**#1: Don't cut corners.**</u> Don't ignore any steps in the process or skip over any of the material – *except for* when I issue a **"Permission Slip to Skip,"** where I am offering modifications based on certain specifics (e.g., you have very young versus older children; you live with your parenting partner versus being a single parent). In these circumstance, I will give you a **Permission Slip to Skip** any piece of that section that does not apply to you or your kids. Otherwise, stick to the process, in order, even when it may seem that certain pieces don't apply to your situation. That is, please trust the process. The creation of an integrated system is one of my *Signature Moves*. The steps in the system work synergistically to create the magic. That is, by definition, a system is a collection of parts that *work together,* not separately. For example, you can't establish Routines but skip over Rules because your children are well-behaved. You still need Rules! If you are blessed with children who are well-behaved, but who just tend to be forgetful or easily-distracted, putting Rules in place for them, as well as for yourself, isn't going to change that. It can only make things better.

<u>**#2: Don't rush it.**</u> I have the system set up so it *can be* done in 28 days – because I *want* you to have the family of your dreams sooner rather than later. But I also want you to feel great about what you are doing. I want you to be able to enjoy seeing and reveling in the new-

found calm in your home. But that doesn't mean that you *must* do it in 28 *consecutive* days. If you need to stop for a few days, just pick up where you left off. As mentioned above, I just want you to stick with it.

The last thing I want is for the *stress-free* system to *add* stress to your life. That would be defeating the purpose, wouldn't it? This is the real world, kids get sick, families go on vacation, there are work deadlines that need to be met. I get it! If something slows you down, don't worry. Put the book down. Leave it on your nightstand and just get back to it as soon as you can. Then, keep going until you get done—no matter how long it takes. Just stay on track and spend any days in between ensuring that you continue to apply the elements you have learned about and applied. It's not a race. It's a journey.

#3: <u>Trust the process.</u> Each aspect of the system has great benefits and will produce positive outcomes you'll begin to see almost immediately. But because it is a *system*, you won't see the greatest transformation until you get to the end when you integrate the individual segments, and everyone is 'on the same page.'

#4: <u>Keep it a secret from your children.</u> As I mentioned, this is another *Signature Move*. DON'T tell your children what you're up to or otherwise indicate that big changes are on the way. This is important enough that I will remind you about it from time to time. Don't worry, I'll be telling you exactly how to initiate and integrate the necessary changes for creating your stress-free home *without* rousing their suspicions or causing a commotion. Keeping it a secret allows you to have the time you need to implement the changes without feeling pressured, having to explain yourself, or being told it won't work. At the end of the book, I'll show you how to conduct a family meeting, which is when you'll tell your children what they need to know. (That will be your final assignment on Day 28, or – preferably – the Sunday after you finish the book!) For now, go into stealth mode. This is our little secret.

#5: If there is another person parenting your child – you'll need to decide whether and when to inform and/or invite them. I hope that doesn't sound too sterile. I simply worded it that way because I know there are a variety of types of households out there. For example, you may be parenting with someone who is supportive and completely 'in the game' with you. Alternatively, you may have a partner that, for whatever reason, they may not be as hands-on as you. Or, you might be a single parent, who has either shared custody with your ex or sole custody of your children.

No matter what your parenting situation is, you need to decide how, or *if*, you'll invite your child's other parent to actively participate in creating your stress-free home. I'm assuming that, since you're reading this, you are the primary caregiver. As such, it is up to you to know how the other parent is likely to respond to your 28-day journey. If there is another person parenting your child, knowing the kind of parent you are dealing with is important in deciding how and *when* (before or after the 28 days) you tell them about the changes that will be taking place.

Every mom I work with asks me about the involvement of the parenting partner and how to handle bringing them onboard or leaving them out of it. Therefore, I'm going to share with you tips and language specific to several scenarios. You'll need to determine how, when, or even if you're going to share what you're up to with your parenting partner. Your approach to this will depend largely on the following factors. This is your first **Permission Slip to Skip!** In this section that follows, read only the information that applies and will be helpful to you.

THE 28-DAY STRESS-FREE FAMILY SYSTEM COMMUNICATION TIPS

How to Communicate with Co-parent(s) Who Are:

- **Onboard** – This means they are supportive, will learn the system, and partner with you to implement and enforce the system. You can include them either by having them go through the system with you step-by-step or just giving them key points. This applies whether you are co-parenting and living in the same home or cooperatively co-parenting in separate homes. If you are in separate homes, the ideal situation for everyone involved would be to create a system that's consistent in both homes. Having the other parent "on board" is obviously the best possible scenario. If this is what you will be working with, go you! It's a great thing to be able to provide your children with two parents who work as a united front.

- **Staying out of the way** – that means they are supportive in that they know there is a problem and they want things to change but, just aren't ready, willing, or able to help you do anything about it. They may not know how or may think it will be too hard. They may even feel like they won't be able to make the necessary commitments to seeing it through. Don't worry. You don't really need them to do anything to help you - as long as they won't do anything to hinder the process. You just need to get them to agree not to interfere, push back, or block your efforts. Just by being present and involved in the day-to-day life of your family, they will either learn the system or know enough about it to be able to slip right in when they can or want to.

- **Invisible** – If you are in a situation where technically you co-parent but, in reality, the other parent is "absent" from parental responsibilities for whatever reason, OR you live in separate homes and you have no communication or relationship with this person, then it is reasonable to assume you are on your own. Move forward as if they are not there. Even if your children spend time with the other parent who is not implementing the system, you just keep at it. Your child will benefit GREATLY from you building a stronger foundation in your home. You cannot make someone else do this in their home if they don't want to, but you can stay strong and consistent on your own. It is even quite possible that when your child's other parent sees the changes that are taking place (and they will if they spend time with your children), they may ask you what, why, and how these changes happened. And if your children are really fortunate, their other parent might actually decide to make these changes in their home, as well.

- **Interfering** – also known as sabotaging. This is the case when, whether they live in the same home or not, they try to block or undo your efforts. If this is your situation, it is going to be best if you go 'stealth mode' on them, too. Keep it to yourself. Just make your changes for you and for your family and don't let this person discourage you! Don't let them win. If they win, you and your children lose.

Speaking of not telling your child's other parent about *what* you are doing…

Based upon the level of involvement and support you have from your child's other parent, you will determine **when** you tell them what you are doing. Should you tell them *before* or *after*?

WHEN TO TELL THEM BEFORE

Tell your parenting partner before you start if you believe they will be all-in, will be willing to help, or will be a silent supporter (on board, out-of-the-way or invisible).

Here are some possible ways to begin and engage in this conversation:

Use their own words to help them understand the need for the system.

What are they complaining about? What are they worried about? What frustrates them about how things are working (or not working) at home? Do they complain because all everyone seems to do is yell? Are they frustrated because the kids are misbehaving?

Whether or not they are justified in feeling this way really doesn't matter right now. Remember, you are just trying to get them to either get on board and support you in this endeavor or to get out of the way, so you can have the stress-free family you want.

For example, if they've complained in the past that you are always "flying off the handle," you can say, "You've mentioned before that I've been flying off the handle a lot lately," and then describe how this has been affecting you, them, and the children. It doesn't matter whether you agree or not that you have *actually been* "flying off the handle". Don't worry about that. It's more important right now that you ask for what you need in a way that gets you what you want.

Introduce the solution.

Once you have described the challenges using their words, introduce the solution. Tell them you have decided to do something that you are sure is going to help and is going to require making a few changes around the home. Highlight how these changes are going to send those frustrations and concerns down the drain and that your home will transform into a happier, calmer, and stress-free place to be. Explain that you'd love to have them help you with it, but that they don't have to. They can just sit back and enjoy the ride if that's what they prefer. Tell them that if they choose not to help, however, that you ask that they respect your decision and not do anything to undermine what you are about to do.

If, for example, they are all for your efforts, but can't, don't want to, or are unable to be an active participant, you can say, "Because our home will be running so smoothly and easily, I'm not going to be so stressed out anymore, so I'll have more patience with you. There's nothing for you to do but enjoy the new-found peace in our home. Doesn't that sound great?"

Or, maybe you can say something like this: "Since we're going to have a nice and relaxed morning Routine, Johnny will get to school on time, with everything he needs for the day, without being flustered and anxious when he gets there. Won't it be nice knowing he's learning to be more responsible? That's just one benefit of the system I'm starting. Isn't that great?"

Get them on board or out of the way.

There's no need to be rude, condescending, or threatening. Just tell them you've 'got this' and that all you ask is that they cooperate—either by getting on board or staying out of your way. When you put it that way, it will be hard for them to say no. Then as you go through the program, let them in on what you are doing, as you do it, and just ask them to support you by hanging back and enjoying the outcome.

At this point I want to remind you that you can do this on your own – it's easy. You do not need anyone's help. It's nice but not necessary. And it is so much easier to do it alone than to do it with someone pushing up against your efforts. So again, your only goal is to get them on board or out of the way, your goal is NOT to try to get them to help!

WHEN TO TELL THEM AFTER

You should use this option if you believe that a discussion with your parenting partner or ex-partner is going to get you nowhere.

If this is your situation, the best thing you can do is to get started without saying anything to anyone. If you are just not on the same page when it comes to parenting but are living together or are in regular communication with them - they won't be able to ignore the fact that things are changing for the better.

Chances are they will make a comment or two or ask if you've noticed what is taking place. When they do, feel free to make a few casual remarks about what you are doing. Your goal should be to acknowledge the fact that they are paying attention to the positive outcome resulting from your efforts…but in a casual way.

Remember: you didn't include them in the first place because you believed you would face opposition to the plan. Keep that in mind and keep it subtle. Make casual comments about things like:

- The fact that you got a note from your child's teacher, complimenting their improved behavior and/or grades.
- How much more relaxed you feel lately.
- How nice and peaceful breakfast with the children has been.

Just be sure your comments don't include anything about The Stress-Free Family System. Then, just like with your children, you can reveal everything on the final day at your family meeting. Waiting until then will make it much easier to 'sell' everyone on the system.

Day 1 Assignment:

- Read and commit to the guidelines.
- Decide if, how, and when you will share The 28-Day Stress-Free Family System with your child's co-parent(s).
- Grab a dedicated journal for working on the book and its assignments.

Okay, that covers all the basics of getting started. But, before we get down to the business of deciding to decide, I want to take a moment to mention that this book will provide you with every step you need to successfully complete the program. However, I also offer a more thorough and guided version of the system. This 'super version' is an online, home study program which includes worksheets, templates, full scripts, and video instruction. In the videos, I give you step-by-step instructions, multiple examples, and scenarios to illustrate how each step is meant to play out, *plus* a hefty dose of encouragement! There is also an option for ongoing mentoring, a community and an option for support with accountability and implementation. If after reading this book and completing the 28-day process, you'd like more support or want to learn the system in its entirety, go to www.thestressfreefamily.com/go.

Now, are you ready to get this show on the road?

Let's do this!

Day 2:
Pillar 1 Routines – Get Acquainted with Pillar 1 of the Stress-Free Family:
ROUTINES

Today's Overview:

- Signature Moves
    - o The advantages of consistency and predictability
    - o A new definition of Routines, which are *Detailed* and *Optimized*
    - o Eight steps to perfect Routines
- What you'll need
    - o Your journal

"When your children are behaving well, and your home is running smoothly, there's a lot of room for fun."

~Madeleine Davis, Author, and Creator
of The 28-Day Stress-Free Family System

Why do I start with Routines? Let me ask you a question. Imagine your kids had effective Routines at home that were really nailed down. That means, your kids knew what to do and when to do it, so they did their Routines without you having to remind them and nag them, without pushback or negotiation. If you imagine your home like that, in terms of a percentage, how much stress would that reduce in your home?

I ask moms that question several times each day. I must've asked that question thousands of times so far. And I always get a crazy high percentage, usually over 70%. WHOA! Moms say they'd have 70% less stress just from nailing down Routines! I've had some moms tell me that 100% of the stress in their home would be reduced if their kids knew what to do and when. Now, I know that that isn't really true. But when a mom tells me that, I know it means a lack of Routines is a really big deal at home. So, I start with Routines because I want you to immediately decrease the stress level in your home. I want you to know how it *feels* to have less stress in your home, and I want you to get excited when you see things changing. Then, once you start seeing the possibilities, you will be motivated to keep going!

And that is exactly the magic of Routines! Routines are sequences of events that make our days run as efficiently as possible, freeing up time and energy to get more out of life. The key is to *design* your household Routines, rather than allow them to happen by default. Then, with practice, your family's Routines will become habits. *You* will get to stop nagging and yelling, and *your kids* will begin to adhere to their Routines automatically!

Routines are helpful to everyone, but they're particularly important for our children because they promote consistency. Consistency provides a strong sense of security, and that sense of security results in your child being more responsible and cooperative.

As adults, we have control over a lot of what goes on in our lives – even though it doesn't always feel like it, right? Not so with children. For them, everything is always changing. Think about it…

- New schools, new teachers, new friends, new classes
- Ever-changing expectations and responsibilities – and more pressure – as they get older
- Ongoing changes in their emotional, mental, and physical development

Children experience these things and much more without any real sense of control over them. Even though these new changes are necessary and offer new opportunities and new experiences, they can be highly stressful.

Because these changes are unavoidable, we should be doing whatever we can at home to make life more predictable for them. Establishing Routines at home provides your children with the security of knowing what to expect. Routines will help them learn to trust their environment and, more importantly, to trust you. It's an added bonus that effective Routines happen to make *our* lives easier (i.e., stress-free!). So, it's a clear win-win.

The 28-Day Stress-Free Family System starts here because effective Routines will immediately reduce stress in your home. Successful Routines will make every part of the day run more smoothly. Imagine everyone in the house knowing *and* doing everything that needs to be done for

- Getting ready and out the door every morning
- Coming home from school
- Transitioning to (and from) activities
- Dinnertime
- Bedtime

Can you imagine it? Every waking hour will become calm instead of chaotic!

Let me ask you this: If Routines at home did nothing else but get you and your children out the door, on time, every morning WITHOUT any yelling, nagging, or anxiety about missing homework or not having anything to wear, would it be worth it to you?

How much of a difference in your attitude would it make? How much more effectively would you be able to tackle the rest of your day?

How much do you think it would help your child's ability to focus and concentrate on their school work? How about how they interact with their friends?

When you start your day off on a calm note, you store up positive energy, reserving it for handling whatever happens after that. When you have energy reserves to do what you *want* to do after you've completed what you *must* do, life is just better all around. In my opinion, that's priceless.

Establishing Routines for the repeated sequences of household activities causes a cycle of behavior…

- Morning Routines get you and your children out of the house without everyone falling apart.
- Leaving the house in a good mood makes you ready to meet the demands of the day.
- Starting the day in a calm manner allows your children to focus on learning and make them more able to behave well at school.
- Coming home to an Afternoon Routine helps kids settle back in, putting things away where they belong and organizes their homework activities.
- Evening Routines relax you and your children because everyone knows what to expect and one step flows easily to the next

- Bedtime Routines eliminate resistance and arguments, helping children (and adults) fall asleep more easily and enjoy better quality sleep.

Rinse and repeat! The next day starts all over again…Routinely… and stress-free.

Before we create your home's stress-free Routines, I want you to understand Routines aren't merely doing the same things every day. Routines are doing the same things, in the same way, at the same time every day. For example, you brush your teeth every morning - but brushing isn't a Routine if you sometimes do it at the sink before breakfast and sometimes you brush your teeth after breakfast standing at your sink, and sometimes you brush your teeth while you double check that the kids haven't fallen back to sleep!

Brushing your teeth is a Routine if you brush them while standing in front of the bathroom sink, right after you eat your breakfast, and before you put your shoes on. In other words, Routines are as much about the sequence of events as they are about the events themselves. When something is done repeatedly, in the same order, our brains begin to prompt us to get ready for the next activity. After a while, our brain tells us to move on to the next linked or anticipated step. "*First*, I do this; *then* I do that".

By creating Routines – that is, doing the same things, at the same time, in the same way – eventually your children won't need to think about it. They'll just do it. And when they 'just do it,' guess who's not reminding, nagging, or yelling. Yep! That would be *you*, Mom!

Over the course of the next few days, you will be learning how to identify which Routines you need to establish in your home, how to create the most effective Routines, and how to train your children to 'fall into' these Routines, anticipating their next natural next step so that the Routines become instinctive.

To do this the *right* way, we need to get very detailed to create the most efficient Routines possible. It's essential to invest the time to get it right, because you don't want to train your kids to follow inefficient Routines. There are a lot of things your children do every single day, but because they aren't detailed, Ordered, and Optimized, chaos and stress have an opportunity to creep in. *The 28 Day Stress-Free Family System* eliminates the stress and chaos by establishing efficient, detailed, Ordered and Optimized Routines.

For example, if sometimes your child packs up their homework for school in the morning and sometimes they pack up their homework at night, that means they're missing a step in their Routine that includes "homework packing" as a step. Without that as a specific, Ordered step, you'll end up with too many, time-wasting double checks in the mornings – or they could head to school without their completed homework. And I'm sure you know what happens next. They're stressed out. They're calling you in a panic. Then YOU have to decide whether it's worth it to add a task to your day (that is, delivering homework to school) or letting them take a zero for the assignment. Both you and your child end up wasting precious time and energy, which creates stress.

Now you may be thinking that it's not a big deal, or that things like that are just a part of life, but they don't have to be. Missing homework or having to call mom will stress your child out and can make it difficult for them to focus on their learning. Plus, missing that one step in their Routine can make the rest of the day feel "off." Even if you homeschool your children, there's still 'homework' that needs to be done. If your children are scrambling around, unsure where they put their homework after completing it, then this is a missing step!

Most moms know they need to create a morning or evening Routine to keep things running smoothly at home. Many moms also embrace the idea and create charts and checklists. Unfortunately, they soon figure out that they don't really work. Usually, they don't address the whole picture, and *that's* why they're not truly effective. Here's the *Signature Move:* If you want to establish Routines that naturally lead to the other elements of a Stress-Free home, you need to follow my eight-step process.

Did "eight-step process" make you panic a little just now? Eight steps may sound like "too much" work, but my process actually breaks it down as simply as possible, for maximum, long-term results. And I'm going to walk you through it. Trust me: It's going to be so worth it! In fact, I think this is a good time to stop and reflect a little more on why Routines are important in your home.

As you move through the eight steps, your initial reaction to some of my advice might lead you to believe that I run my home like an institution. For example, I'm going to ask you to follow your kids around with a timer (secretly, though!), and to give them *very* detailed, step-by-step instructions in the beginning. I want to assure you that nothing could be further from the truth.

Adopting these Pillars in your home years will allow the atmosphere in your house to become much warmer and calmer. You'll find that you'll become closer as a family. Why? Because you'll be making room to *be a family* instead of a collection of different people, going in all different directions, trying to cooperate but often getting in one another's way. Routines and Rhythms (next chapter!) will streamline all the stuff you *have to do*, leaving you white space to get to do the things you *want to do*. You'll get to spend more *quality* time together. You'll all be much happier when you have time and energy left over to participate in activities each of you enjoy!

Plus, think about the amount of time you are away from your family – for example, when you're at work and they're at school – versus the amount of time that you are with them. Work and school are obligations – more have-to-dos. You don't have to count the hours and do the math. Just come up with a general sense of the percentage of time you are home versus work and school. Got it?

I'm guessing that you estimated that you're home a third to half of the time of your waking hours – at least on your weekdays. Now take that "home" time, your *family* time, and think about how much of it you and your family are busy doing the have-to-dos of living in and running your household. Are you noticing that those have-to-do tasks that eat away at your precious "home time" are the *Routine* tasks of the day? Have you ever taken the time to calculate just how much of your waking hours are spent dealing with the logistical and operational aspects of parenting? It's amazing how much time that part of our job eats up! Well, guess what! Having solid Routines for you and your family helps you to "buy back" some of that lost home time. For example, you may not spend every minute together during your respective morning Routines, but you aren't in one another's way or having to stop *your* Routine (stress!) to help the kids with theirs. And when you do cross paths as you prepare for the day, everyone is calm and happy to see one another. Plus, you'll get to sit down to breakfast together instead of throwing a bowl of cereal at them and cramming a protein bar in your mouth as you're walking out the door! Basically, solid Routines *add to* your family time by allowing your family to enjoy one another while you are completing your "have-to-dos" at home. They take the "grind" out of the daily grind!

You don't have to just take my word for it. My Stress-Free Family mom Kelli had this to say about the system: "It's crazy to think that changing the ways we get things done could have such a huge impact on us. But it's like we've turned into different people! My family not only gets everywhere on time now and the house is less cluttered and more orderly, but we get along so much better. We actually *like* each other more! Airtight Routines allow time for things like family game nights, family outings, and important conversations. But what's more is that even when we're simply plodding through our day-to-day tasks – our Routines – there's a "lightness" in the house we didn't have "before." Now that we're an "after" family, we're not making each other crazy with things like scrambling for lost socks or last-minute homework checks. Instead, we talk and joke around while we're getting ready for the day or as we're getting settled in after school. By cutting out the daily stress, we've made room for joy, laughter, and even quiet time for Mom! I finally stopped feeling 'like a bad mom' because the system works for me *and* my kids."

Doesn't that sound fabulous? Can you imagine that kind of atmosphere in your home? Well, get excited about this transformation occurring in *your* home because you are about to master Pillar One, Routines and you'll be enjoying results as soon as you introduce them to their kids. And then we'll learn and mix in FOUR more Pillars! The Pillars work together, so you won't just be *adding* positive results each time you adopt a Pillar. Your outcomes are going to *multiply* into so much family goodness, you're going to amaze yourself! By the time we get through Rhythms, Rules, Rewards, and Revolutionize, you're going to have a home like Kelli's!

Day 2 Assignment:

- Review the eight steps to effective Routines that we will be working on in the days ahead. I want you to get familiar with them so that you know what to expect and so you can see that it's not as complicated as it may sound!

Eight Steps to Effective Routines:

1. Identify Transitions: Transitions are the material shifts that occur in your child's day. Usually, these are when they wake up, come home from school and go to sleep. NOTE: Whenever your child Routinely leaves the home and when they enter the home would be a Transition. The very first step is to identify all of those Transitions because each Transition time needs a separate Routine. I start with Transitions because those are the times in the day when things tend to fall apart.

2. Detail the Steps: We list all of the steps that are needed to get the Routine/Transition completed in a smooth and timely

fashion. What *should* occur for a smooth Transition is probably very different from what IS happening in your home now. This step brings clarity to what should be happening, when it should be happening, and during which Transition all tasks should occur.

3. <u>Timing</u>: Determine how long each of these steps should take. This is an area where a lot of Routines go awry. Most moms don't know how long it actually takes their child to do something. Enough time needs to be given to complete the step successfully, but not so much time as to create an opportunity for dawdling!

4. <u>Optimize</u>: This refers to *Ordering* and *Clustering* every step in the Routine. That is, steps are placed in a logical order, and they are "Clustered" by room. For example, all the steps that occur in the bathroom during a Transition should be grouped together while in the bathroom to minimize time wasted by moving from room to room and to avoid possibilities for distraction.

5. <u>Create the Checklist</u>: – We put it all together in a neat checklist that includes all steps, in order, Clustered by room. Because you have also carefully considered the time needed, you can determine what time each Routine must begin because you know what time it needs to end (e.g., what time the kids leave for school), and you know how much time the Routine will take.

6. <u>Communicate</u>: You need to let your children know what to do and when. In other words, it's time to roll out their new Routines, using carefully designed messages that help them "connect the dots" and without letting on that this is Mom's new "system."

7. <u>Support with Reminders</u>: Remind them of the steps and sequence of the Routine, using as few words as possible, as few

times as necessary. Gradually taper off your support. Your goal here is to be able to pass the baton - not hold onto it the whole race.

8. <u>Practice makes Progress</u>: Keep at it and be patient. As they practice their Routines, it won't be long before they get into the flow and their Routines become their "new normal." For you, that new normal will be more grace and ease at home!

Day 3:
Pillar 1 Routines – Step 1: Identify Transitions

Today's Overview:

- *Signature Moves*
  - o Creating Routines for *all* your family's Transitions
  - o Keeping it a secret from the kids
- What you'll need
  - o Your journal for today's assignment

"The secret of your future is hidden in your daily routine."

~Mike Murdock, American Singer-Songwriter

Now that you're clear on what Routines are (and what they are not), today's task is to determine which Routines you need. *Signature Move* alert! A success factor of my system is that I prescribe creating Routines for every *Transition* that takes place in your home. Transitions are when things *happen* – when you're moving from one stage in your day to the next. Today we start with Step One in creating effective Routines by identifying the Transitions in your home, as each needs its own Routine. Here are some examples to further clarify Transitions and their connections to Routines.

In school, kids *Transition* from one class to the next. That Transition has a *Routine:* The bell rings, students pack their things, and the teacher dismisses them. Then, within a specified period of time, they move to the next classroom, take their seats, and wait for instruction to begin.

At home, you *Transition* from sleeping to waking and getting ready for the day, from home to school, from school to home, and so forth. Most moms, if they have Routines at all, only have morning and evening/bedtime Routines. But we *need* Routines for *all* the major Transitions in a home: when the kids wake up and leave for school, when they come home from school and when they get ready for bed. So, *every* home needs Routines for mornings, after school, and bedtime – so that is where we will start. Additional Routines may be needed for Transitions like going to afterschool/weekend activities, dinnertime, and bath time, depending on your home and ages of your children.

Here's why my approach to Routines is a *Signature Move:* This first step of identifying and acknowledging the Transitions in your home isn't even on most people's radar. But taking the time to do this is extremely important because it's in the Transitions that havoc usually shows up. Creating Routines around Transitions will immediately bring a sense of calm and ease to your home.

When my client Jill first started working with me, she thought she had pretty good morning and bedtime Routines because her kids didn't fuss that much at night and mornings were manageable. Where she really struggled was after school when her kids would come home, and everything would just fall apart. She'd constantly be reminding her kids to return their lunch boxes to the kitchen or yelling at them to put their shoes away when they kicked them off at the door. And getting them to do their homework was a huge battle. It was extremely stressful and chaotic. And you know what stress and chaos does to a mom? It makes her feel like *a bad mom*, which is heartbreaking for every mom in the world.

When we began working on Routines, she realized that by not looking at the Afterschool Transition, she missed a huge opportunity to have her children RESET. Once Jill established after school Routines – Routines that not only included each of these steps but specified when they occurred, in order – her afternoons with her kids became a lot more relaxed and even fun! She also realized after going through the eight Steps of Creating Effective Routines, that her Morning and Evening Routines could be greatly improved. Soon, her bedtimes became calm and relaxed. And while her mornings were already "manageable," after she Optimized the morning Routines, she found they had the time to sit together at breakfast as a family. She really enjoyed starting their off day in that way and the "bad mom" feelings disappeared.

To repeat, your family needs morning, afternoon/after school, and evening Routines. If your child comes home from school and then departs again for an afterschool activity, that would be an additional Transition, requiring its own Routine. Each and every Transition requires a Routine to be built around it. But because the morning and evening hours tend to be problematic for most people, we are going to work on creating morning, afternoon, and evening Routines. If your family has additional Routines, add as necessary.

Permission Slip to Skip: Special note for homeschooling families:

Even though your children aren't going to and from a traditional school, you still need Routines for any times they leave home and come back. Also, even though they are not changing locations for their school day, they need a Routine for *mentally* Transitioning to the schooling part of the day. In fact, this Routine might be even more important for homeschoolers than it is for kids leaving for school. There needs to be a clear shift in everyone's mind that you're shifting from "home" or "family" mode into "education" mode.

Day 3 Assignment:

In your journal, make a list of all the Transitions in your home for which you need to create a Routine. Again, you will definitely need a morning, after school, and evening, but add any other major Transitions that happen for your family. Don't worry yet about creating the Routines for these Transitions! Just ensure you know what Transitions you have and when they occur.

Day 4:
Pillar 1 Routines – Step 2:
Detail the Steps for Each Routine

Today's Overview:

- *Signature Moves*
  - o Creating Routines for *all* of your family's Transitions
  - o Keeping it a secret from the kids
- What you'll need
  - o Your journal for the assignment

"The difference between something good and something great is attention to detail."

~ Charles Swindoll

Remember the story I told you about my wakeup call – the day I decided to decide to do something about my situation? The day I wore two different shoes to walk my kids to school? Well here's the deal…. that night, I decided that from that moment on, I would lay out my clothes and shoes the night before, so no matter what was going on in the morning, that would be one thing I didn't need to think about.

If I would have had effective Routines instead of just getting things done by yelling, grabbing, scurrying, and scrambling - the 2 different shoes incident would never have happened. A Routine would have included laying out my clothes the night before. But an effective Routine would have included DETAILS including choosing matching shoes! And when you have effective Routines like laying out your clothes the night before, that leaves you time in the morning to 'indulge' in a mirror-check to make sure that what you select the night before is something that will contribute to making you feel good about yourself all day. THAT is why we need Step 2 in this process of establishing Routines:

Detailing the Steps or Tasks that Need to Happen During Each Transition

A loose Routine instructs your children to go to the bathroom or just to get ready for the day. But until all the actions that occur in the bathroom become linked in their brains, it won't become a successful Routine. They will most likely use the restroom, leave the bathroom to do something else, wait their turn (waste time) to go back into the bathroom to take care of personal hygiene, leave again, and then possibly 'need' to go back one more time before leaving the house. YIKES! That kind of Routine simply has too much wasted time and too much potential for forgetting things.

A better Routine would include each of the bathroom steps – use the toilet, wash hands, brush teeth, wash face, etc. – *while* they are in there. One trip.

Doing this has a great deal of validity. You wouldn't believe how many moms I work with whose teenagers have left for school without brushing their teeth because they simply forgot! Teenagers forgetting to brush their teeth? Seriously? But it happens because it's not part of their Routine.

For this step in the process, I want you to take your time to really think about every step required for each of the Routines/Transitions you've identified – and to write them down in your notebook. Be thorough and don't rush through this, but don't worry about grouping or ordering the steps, as I did with the bathroom example above, just yet. We'll get to that later. Remember, Routines are the foundational cornerstone for the rest of this system, so they need to be solid and complete. It's even quite possible that it will take you a few days to capture every detail of each Routine in your journal. That's okay. It is more important that you get this right than it is for you to get it done today.

For example, what might be happening now when they get home from school is nothing but playtime or screen time. But what you *want* to happen when they come home from school is for them to grab a quick, healthy snack and do any homework they have. And that's what we are about to change. That's what this Routine creation process is for.

You will undoubtedly be able to think of all the big steps quickly and easily. The *Signature Move* that makes this work is including all of the details and not missing any steps, no matter how small. Remember: your children are just children. They don't see the need for taking their wet or muddy shoes off at the door on their own. They need you to explain to them *why* walking around the house in wet shoes is *not* a great idea. When you establish and teach them these things through Routines, they will learn and comply without any hassle.

Identify what you want to happen and write it down in detail. If after school, you want your child to hang up their jacket when they walk in the door, include that. If you want them to take their shoes off at the door, add it to the list.

Make the list, check it twice. Set it aside for a day or two, then come back to it and go through it with a fine-toothed comb to make sure you haven't missed anything. You can even take a couple of days or so to mentally follow your kids around the house, making notes about what they do versus what you want them to do. Then ask yourself, "What small steps did I miss?"

Here are some additional questions to assist you in making sure you get the detailed list you need:

- What's not working out or falling through the cracks?
- What have your children forgotten to do in the past?
- Do they sometimes forget to bring their lunch to school?
- Do they sometimes forget to brush their teeth?
- Do they forget to pack their homework?
- What things result in delays or arguments? (e.g., picking out clothes or shoes, finding their homework)

Make sure those tasks make it to your list. Break each Transition down, step by step, one little detail at a time.

I'll give you another example. Amy, another of my Stress-Free Family moms, had an afterschool "Routine" for her kids. They'd come home, put their coats and shoes away, and have an afternoon snack before starting their homework. Sounds pretty good, right? Well, the kids were missing the step "clean up after yourself "after snack time. Amy needed to make space for preparing dinner, so she'd either end up cleaning the kitchen mess herself or yelling at her kids to come back and clean up after themselves. Both outcomes made her feel angry and frustrated. So, she added "clean up your snack" to the kids' Routine, and she was able to eliminate that nuisance from *her* dinner prep Routine. Another missing step was "pack up homework". Sometimes, in their excitement to run outside and play after they were done with their homework, her kids would leave their notebooks on the kitchen table instead of putting them back into their backpacks. Once these steps were added to the afterschool Routine, Amy didn't have to feel angry and frustrated, anymore. Those simple additions have allowed her to feel the calm of being a "together mom."

So, think about it. What are the differences between what is happening in your home now and what you would like to happen during your children's Transitions? I think it's safe to say (since you are read-

ing this book) that there are a significant number of differences between the two. But it's time to get excited because it's all about to improve – a lot!

Are you ready to get started? Great!

Day 4 Assignment:

- Write the name of each Routine/Transition (e.g., "Morning," "Afterschool") you need in your home at the top of separate pages in your journal.

- For each Routine, record the steps required for that Transition, being as detailed as possible.

Day 5:
Pillar 1 – Routines Step 3: Timing

Today's Overview

- *Signature Moves*
  - o Timing steps of Routines
- What you'll need
  - o A timer
  - o Your journal – where you've recorded detailed steps for each Routine

---

"Time passes irrevocably."

~Virgil, Ancient Roman Poet

Okay, so now that you know **what** it is you want them to do – every little step needed for each Transition within your Routine – it's time for you to determine the '***hows***' of each step. We'll begin the "how" process by considering the amount of time required for each step in the Routine.

Time is a funny thing. Most people don't really know how long a task *actually* takes to do. Usually, people underestimate how much time they need – which makes them late. Most people, especially children, don't know how *long* 'five minutes' FEELS like!

Timing their steps is very important for three reasons:

1. It's important to know how long a task takes to do so that you know how much time you reasonably need to get it done. In order to have realistic expectations for getting out the door on time or to bed on time, we need to know how long things really take, so we can know when the process must begin. This is called "reverse engineering."

2. Once we realize how long something really takes, we might make the decision to move things around, doing them at a time that makes more sense. (That's called Optimizing, and we'll get to that on Day 6!)

3. If your children get easily distracted or start dawdling or slacking off, you will need to start using timers to keep them focused on the tasks at hand.

When figuring out how much time to designate for each step, you will have to actually time yourself and/or your children to complete this step of the process. It's a *Signature Move* to time your children's steps precisely. But remember—don't let them know what you are doing. This is still our little secret, so you need to do this in stealth mode. You can just use the stopwatch function on your smartphone!

If it really is a tiny task like taking a vitamin, just write down one minute. Some tasks, like brushing teeth, are easy to time. But others, such as getting dressed and eating breakfast will depend on several factors including a) the age of the child, b) the time of year (i.e., number of layers required due to weather, and c) what they are eating. Because of this, I suggest you "time" them over several days. If over three days it takes your child an average of eight minutes to get dressed, then write down eight minutes. Just start today to begin to see what is realistic for your child.

As you determine the amount of time for each step in the Routine, remember that you need to do so based on the amount of time it

SHOULD realistically take. That is, if you see them dawdling and getting distracted, either don't include this in your time allotment or note that it's an opportunity for improvement. However, don't worry about this too much at this point. Tomorrow, we're going to be addressing how to save time by completing the Routines most efficiently.

One of my clients, who was first skeptical about timing tasks, told me this task was eye-opening. Although Lynn knew that time was occasionally wasted in the mornings, doing things like hunting for lost socks, she had assumed that the *Routine* tasks just took as long as they took. When she started observing her kids more closely, she realized that tasks like her kids getting dressed took a lot longer than they needed to because of distractions or last-minute wardrobe changes. On the flip side, Lynn also noticed that she'd been rushing them through some morning items when they really needed a few more minutes to complete the task correctly, the first time. Adjusting the time allotment for these steps accordingly allowed for a more effective, natural flow to their mornings, Adjusting the times to get things right saved a lot of "do over" time!

Once you have your time allotments figured out, you can record them alongside each Routine step you recorded on Day 4 of your journal.

Again, please don't just guess the times. Observe your children for a few days and note accurate times.

I understand that there are times that you may not be home when your children Transition. For example, maybe you work, and you are not there when they come home in the afternoon. If this is the case in your home, you are going to have to bring their caregiver on board with you. Tell them what you're working on and ask them to watch and note the amount of time each child spends on each task in the morning and/or afterschool Transitions, as well as to identify areas that need improvement (e.g., dawdling and procrastination). *Don't forget to tell the caregiver that this is a SECRET!* They can't say anything to your children about what they are doing for you.

Day 5 Assignment:

- Stealthily use your timer app on your phone, or carefully keep track with a clock, noting the amount of time each child needs to complete the steps in his or her Routines.

- Note those times next to each step you recorded in your journal on Day 4.

Day 6:
Pillar 1 Routines Step 4: Optimize

Today's Overview:

- *Signature Move*
  - o Optimized Routines are Clustered and Ordered
- What you'll need
  - o Your journal

"We are all tasked to balance and optimize ourselves."

~Mae Jemison, American engineer, physician, and NASA astronaut

Once you've completed the timing step, it's time to move on to *Optimizing* your Routines. To Optimize means to enhance, augment, boost, and improve. When speaking in terms of Optimizing your time and Transitions, you will be taking a day to make any necessary additions or subtractions to the Transition steps you've listed thus far, as well reordering any of the tasks where it will be beneficial.

Just as you (or your child) needs to put pants on before shoes to get dressed efficiently, most processes tend to have a logical order to them. However, we often don't think about the natural order and can even end up doing them out of this logical order, if we're not paying attention. But we're paying attention now! When we do things in the most efficient order, we save time and energy, and we're less likely to forget required steps. Everything gets done, and in a timely fashion, and chaos and scrambling become a thing of the past.

When you not only *order* tasks but add my *Signature Move* of *Clustering* tasks, your Routines start really going off without a hitch. Clustering is grouping tasks within a Routine by the room of your home where they need to occur; a *Signature Move* of The 28-Day Stress-Free Family system.

To Cluster tasks, you group them by room (or area) of your home where they take place.

I've already given you an example of a Clustered portion of the morning Routine – what happens in the bathroom upon waking. If your child is headed straight to the bathroom upon waking, it makes sense to perform *all* the bathroom-related tasks while they are already in that room: Use the toilet, wash and dry hands, brush teeth, wash face, wipe down sink. DONE in the bathroom. No need to go back.

Consider how much more efficient that is than going to the bathroom to use the toilet and wash hands, then heading to the kitchen for breakfast, and *then* heading *back* to the bathroom to brush teeth. Moving from room to room is wasting precious time – and providing the opportunity to dawdle or get distracted. A minute to move from place to place may seem like a little thing. But if you lose a minute or two between several steps within your Routine, it adds up and increases the opportunity that you and your children will get behind schedule, have to scramble, and be stressed about the Transition. Not doing this creates opportunities for distraction and dawdling. And returning to rooms multiple times also increases the chance that your child will leave something behind that they will have to go back to retrieve. So, besides, giving you a margin of a few minutes to spend some quality time together, it also eliminates all that dawdling and distraction.

Your job for today is to determine how the steps in your Routine can be Clustered by the room where they take place and then re-ordering them in an efficient sequence that will take place in that location.

Day 6 Assignment:

- Go back to your journal where you recorded the Routine steps and the amount of time each takes. Start a new page for each Transition where you'll write down the *Optimized* Routine.
- Cluster tasks within each Routine by the room of the house your child needs to visit (e.g., bedroom, bathroom, kitchen).
- Within each room, order the Clustered tasks, logically and efficiently.

Day 7:
Pillar 1 Routines – Bonus *Signature Moves*

Today's Overview:

- Signature Moves
  - o Tomorrow Box
  - o Set mornings up for success by starting the night prior
  - o Include Contributions

"Light tomorrow with today."

~ Elizabeth Barrett Browning

We're interrupting our steps in the eight-step Routine process to introduce some *Signature Moves* that you are going to need to add to the Optimized Routines you've recorded in your journal before you move on to step five.

I know, I know. I asked you to do all that work in detailing your Routines, only to tell you that they're not complete without my key steps. I promise (pinky swear!) that these additions are going to be simple and pay huge dividends in your home!

In addition, you'll need to make a plan to find or buy an item you'll need that's essential for when you begin to introduce Routines to your kids. I call it a "Tomorrow Box," and it's a *Signature Move*. In fact, the Tomorrow Box is one of the KEY tools that makes The 28-Day Stress-Free Family System a success. For today, we're just going to go over the need for Tomorrow Boxes, and how they will be incorporated into your Routines.

Signature Move: The Tomorrow Box (or Basket)

A Tomorrow Box or Basket is a container a child can carry that will hold all the items they need to get through their day. My kids named these Tomorrow Boxes because "It's like having tomorrow in a box." But you and your family may end up with a different name for them if you wish. But throughout the book, I'll refer to it as the Tomorrow Box. The Tomorrow Box is the cornerstone of the Stress-Free Family System – again, it's a *Signature Move*. It's used as an easy way to corral everything that needs to move from the children's bedroom to the front door and back again, each day, in a simple, efficient, and organized way.

The Tomorrow Box is the "home" for the items your child needs on a daily basis. Each evening, the children will pack everything they need for the next day into the Tomorrow Box and keep it in a designated place (ideally in their bedrooms). In the morning, they bring the Tomorrow Box to the front door to ensure everything is ready to go out that door with them when it's time to leave.

Therefore, you will need a separate one for each child. The Tomorrow Box must be light-weight and easy to carry, as your child will be moving it between its two locations (bedroom and front door), with all their stuff in it, daily. It should be large enough to hold and carry everything they need for the day. I usually recommend a light-colored plastic basket to be used for this because plastic is light-weight and easy to keep clean. I suggest a light color because that makes it easier to see what is inside (e.g., your children aren't as apt to overlook something lying in the bottom of it). You'll need to either buy or re-purpose something you have in your home already to use for their Tomorrow Boxes. The criteria are simply that it fits in its two locations and that your child can carry it when it's full.

<u>Pro tip</u>: Get each child a different color Tomorrow Box, so you and they can easily identify which belongs to whom. You may want to also consider using a color coding system for related items. For exam-

ple, if your daughter has a purple lunch box and your son's is green, you may want to buy Tomorrow Boxes (and other items) to "match." Color coding is another *Signature Move* I use in my home to keep the three boys' items straight very easily.

Signature Move alert! You may typically think that a successful day starts in the morning, but to set that morning up for success, you really need to start the night before. Therefore, I want you to look at your evening Routine and add "Pack Up Tomorrow Box" as a step where it makes sense for your family. Then we'll talk about what we do with it in the morning and add it to the Morning Routine.

The steps for prepping the Tomorrow Box for the next day must be added to your Evening Routine. Specifically, your child is going to put *everything* they need for the following day into that Tomorrow Box – tomorrow's outfit and shoes and their backpack (which contains their completed homework). If your child goes to an afterschool activity, I suggest a separate drawstring bag that will hold any other items they will need tomorrow for that activity. You may have "get dressed" and "put your shoes on" listed in your Morning Routine, but you need to add "Add tomorrow's outfit and shoes to the Tomorrow Box" to your Evening Routine. Making all clothing decisions the night before results in a much more streamlined morning. And making sure that you have every part of your uniform for your afterschool activity ready means no more scrambling for ballet tights or a sports jersey!

To be clear, all of the following must be placed in the Tomorrow Box:

- Tomorrow's clothing, including outfit, socks, shoes, and any additional accessories.
- School backpack, including completed homework and any other materials that need to be taken to school tomorrow.
- Items for afterschool activities, ideally in a separate bag.

This will be made very clear when we begin to introduce the Routines to your kids. For now, just add "bring your tomorrow box to the door" in your kids' Morning Routines. It should follow the "getting dressed" step.

As I mentioned, the Tomorrow Boxes will "live" in two places within your home, so you need to designate those spots. One spot should be near the door where it will "live" during the day. This is where the Tomorrow Box will be emptied in the morning when they go to school and will be waiting for them when they get home from school. You also need to identify a spot in their bedrooms where the Tomorrow Boxes will be packed up for the next day and waiting for them when they wake up. Got it? One Tomorrow Box for each child. Two places each box will 'live' – one by the front door (or wherever you leave the house, such as the door out to the garage) and one in their bedroom.

The concept of the Tomorrow Box – and how it moves from place to place – may sound onerous or weird to you at first. But I'm going to ask you to trust me yet again. The Tomorrow Box is a primary reason for the success of this system. You will soon begin to LOVE your Tomorrow Box.

1. It makes preparing for the next day very purposeful. They will need to think it through

2. It will be easy to get dressed in the morning because everything is in one place,

3. It will be easy to make sure they have everything they need for the day when they leave in the morning because when they leave, the Tomorrow Box will be empty!

It will be easy to carry things back and forth in your home, so no more shoes at the front, notebooks in the kitchen and jackets on the floor. One trip is all it takes! The Tomorrow Box is a powerhouse.

Signature Move: Add "Contributions" to Routines

In The Stress-free Family System, we use the word, "Contributions" instead of chores. I choose not to use the word 'chores' because I think it's important for children, in an age-appropriate way, to Contribute to the home and understand that they are a valuable and valued member of the family. You may want to consider activities in the home that your child can perform that keep the house tidy and running smoothly. Fifteen minutes a day of Contributions are recommended for each child. This can be done in 5- to 10-minute increments or all at once, depending upon the age and ability of the child. Contributing helps them to learn to be independent, self-sufficient, and responsible. Making Contributions gives them a sense of pride (the good kind).

If you prefer to use another word in place of Contributions, such as chores, tasks, jobs, or duties, that's fine. It's your home and your system. Using your values and beliefs to construct your Routines, Rules, and other Pillars of this system is what will make it work best for your family. As I said, I prefer using the word Contributions because I think it has a more positive connotation than chores.

Regardless of what you call it, I **strongly encourage** you to include Contributions in your Routines. Children need them, for a number of reasons, including:

- Learning important life skills
- Instilling responsibility, self-respect, and accomplishment
- Encouraging strong and positive work-ethic
- Teaching respect for personal property, theirs and others'

Deciding who does what and whether or not these tasks rotate between children is also up to you. You need to be conscious of making sure the things they are expected to do are age-appropriate AND that you first teach them how to do the task properly. Kids aren't born knowing how to wipe down a counter properly or how to load a dishwasher!

At my house, we use a Contributions Chart with a rotating cycle, which is separate from their daily Routines, and where each child has a different Contribution each day. If that sounds good to you – great! Try that. If you choose to do it differently, that's also perfectly fine. You know what's best for your family. However, if you want to assign a specific Contribution as the sole responsibility of one child, add that Contribution to the child's Routine.

Day 7 Assignment:

- Add the details about filling the Tomorrow Box for the next day to your child's Evening Routine (e.g., add tomorrow's clothes; insert backpack) in your journal.

- Add "Take Tomorrow Box to your bedroom" to the Evening Routine.

- Add "Bring Tomorrow Box to the front door" (or the alternate, designated place) to your child's Morning Routine.

- Add "Double check that your Tomorrow Box is empty before you leave for school" as a last step in the Morning Routine.

- Add "15 minutes of Contributions" to each child's Afternoon or Evening Routine, according to your needs, if you choose to begin this practice. (Or add the name of the specific Contribution to be performed to the Routine.)

Day 8:
Pillar 1 Routines –
Step 5: Create Your Checklists

Today's Overview

- Signature Moves
  - o Reusable Routines Checklists
- PRO TIPS
- What you'll need
  - o Plastic sheet protectors
  - o Dry erase markers, at least one for each child

"Life is too complicated not to be orderly."

~ Martha Stewart, American businesswoman, writer,
and lifestyle personality

That quote is so appropriate here, as we're getting back to our eight steps, and we're in the thick of getting all of our families' stuff in order so we can UN-complicate our lives!

In becoming more orderly in our approach to parenting, we've identified our Transitions, listed the steps for each – including the all-important *Signature Moves* of Tomorrow Boxes and Contributions – timed, Clustered, and sequenced them efficiently. Now it's time to start taking action! We're going to formalize your Routines and begin practicing them with your kids – but we're still doing it in stealth mode! On Days 9 and 10, I'm going to tell you how to get your kids started on their Routines without mentioning "Routines" or letting on that Mom is "up to something."

Today, you're going to take the Optimized Routines you created in your journal and type and print out (or neatly handwrite on separate pieces of paper) each Routine for each child. Ideally, you'll include a checkbox next to each item, so your kids can later check each item off the checklists.

The *Signature Move* is printed Routines that don't get messed up AND are reusable because we turn them into "whiteboards" by slipping them into **plastic sheet protectors.** It's not imperative to get them today, as your children won't be working with these printed Routines until a few days from now. However, you will need at least two sheet protectors for Routines for each child. Into one sheet protector, you will slide the Morning and Afternoon Routines, back to back. In the other, you will insert the Evening Routine. If you have a fourth Routine (e.g., afterschool activity), it can be placed back to back with the Evening Routine.

Each child will also need a **dry erase marker** for checking off tasks on their Routines Checklists. You may want to color code the marker for each child to coordinate with their Tomorrow Boxes (and backpacks, water bottles, lunch boxes, etc. – whatever you've decided to color code!). At the end of the day, your kids will be able to swipe their Routine checklist clean, and it will be ready to reuse again at the start of the Morning Routine!

Remember: We are still in Top Secret mode – you're not yet sharing these with your kids!

Note that you can purchase page protectors and dry erase markers where office or school supplies are sold, including discount stores, dollar stores, office supply stores, and even craft stores. Remember, the page protectors serve two purposes:

- To protect the checklists.
- To serve as a dry erase 'boards' for these lists, allowing your children to reuse the same list multiple times.

Later, we will add the Routines Checklists and markers to the To-morrow Boxes. Handling your children's Routines in this way will make it so easy for you to manage their checklists daily and for when you need to change their Routine. When you need to add, subtract, or reorder a Routine, simply slide the paper out, write up a new Routine on a fresh piece of paper, and slide it back in.

PRO TIP: For smaller children who do not read, you can start with images. You can easily find pictures on the internet that symbolize the steps in their Routines.

And here's another PRO TIP: Don't worry that you may have to buy a pack of sheet protectors containing a dozen or more when you only need a couple for your kids' Routines. You're going to fall in love with them! I've learned so many other uses for sheet protectors from the clever moms I've worked with. You can use them for your own Routines (e.g., weekend cleaning), meal planning, recipes you've printed, grocery shopping lists, and so on!

Before we go on to the final step of actually implementing these Routines with your kids, I want to give you a few last words of advice. Okay, so it's a few more than just a few, but….

- Remember that the Routines Checklists are adaptable to your situation. Don't be afraid to personalize them. For example, some children don't have any homework. If this is the case in your house, switch those areas out with things like reading time, exercise, hobby time, and a little one-on-one time with you.

- Don't forget to include after-school activity items to be added to the Tomorrow Box when they are adding their clothes for the next day – it needs to be part of a Routine.

- If your child is younger or needs more specific direction, then you will need to add more details — meaning more steps. For example, "shower" might be a single step for an older child. A younger child will need to be directed to the specific steps that showering requires, such as get your pajamas, grab a towel from the linen cabinet, wash hair and body, dry off, put on PJs, hang up towel, put today's clothes in the hamper.

- **LAST BUT NOT LEAST:** Don't neglect to ensure your children have plenty of downtime or free time to just play and be children.

Day 8 Assignment:

- Type and print (or handwrite) each Routine on a separate piece of paper.

- Insert Morning and Afternoon Routine Checklists back to back into one sheet protector.

- Insert the Evening Routine Checklist and child's fourth Routine Checklist (if applicable) back to back into a second page protector.

NOTE: If you don't already have the page protectors, it's no sweat. Just plan to have them – and the dry erase markers – by Day 11 when you'll be sharing them with your kids and adding them to their Tomorrow Boxes.

Day 9:
Pillar 1 Routines – Step 6: Communicate (Part 1 of 2)

Today's Overview

- *Signature Moves*
  - o Sprinkling
  - o Front- and Back-linking
  - o Rolling our Routines *while* staying in 'stealth mode'
- What you'll need
  - o Your journal – for planning what you'll say
  - o Tomorrow Boxes – will be introduced tomorrow (Day 10)

"Raise your words, not voice. It is rain that grows flowers, not thunder."

~ Rumi, 13th-century Persian Sunni Muslim poet, jurist, Islamic scholar, theologian, and Sufi mystic

Today's the day! After all the hard work you put into creating detailed and Optimized (Ordered and Clustered) Routines, you get to begin 'rolling them out' to your kids. You have done all your "painstaking preparation," and now you get to begin to see the results of your decision to decide to make things better!

You have identified all your Transitions and created a Routine around all that has to be accomplished for each Transition. You have also taken those steps and figured out the best, most efficient way to get them all completed consistently. Your Tomorrow Boxes are ready, and you have your Routines checklists in hand.

I have yet another "stealth" reminder for you! Although you are introducing the Tomorrow Box(es) to your kids and you have a check-list, we're still keeping this under wraps. In a couple of days, you'll share the checklists with them, but for now, they're just for you. You might be wondering how you can be in TOP SECRET mode - yet sharing new ways of Transitioning with your kids. I have that sorted out for you. In the material that follows, I will not be *describing* how to introduce Tomorrow Boxes and how to start the Routines without mentioning "Routines." Instead, I am going to share a *script* of exactly how to make changes while still flying under your kids' radar. Take the script and use it and adapt it to your specific needs. Then sit back and enjoy the results!

Two things before we dive in. First, getting your kids started on your new, effective Routines requires two, carefully worded days of explanation, which is why we're taking two days for "communicate," Step 6 of Routines. Note that we want to begin to introduce these con-cepts to our kids on two, *consecutive days*. Therefore, please make sure you will be able to do that before beginning. It's better to wait until you are certain you can walk through the Routines on two days, back to back, then it is for you to rush into it!

Next, you will notice I use terms like "Sprinkle," "Front-Linking" and "Back-Linking" in my description of what to say. These are im-portant concepts – and *Signature Moves* of The 28-Day Stress-Free Parenting System. What I mean by these terms should become clear as you read through the example script. For example, I use "sprinkling" because it doesn't come off as "Rules" or "instructions," which can lead to eye-rolling and pushback. Sprinkling is just information that high-lights the benefits – *to them* – of what we're doing. Through those ben-efits, you gain their cooperation without coercion. Front- and back-linking steps in the process help our kids to link related steps in their minds to make the flow of our Routines become second-nature.

Okay, *now* we're ready! I'm sitting here in my "director's chair" and giving you your directions to effectively implement your first day of Routines with your kids. I'm giving you the step-by-step formula that works. Review the formula and thoroughly understand it. When you actually speak it to your kids, you'll want to have it down pat. That is, you will likely want to script what you will say, but you don't want to be *reading* it to your kids. You want to be able to deliver it naturally. You'll see that for each segment of each Routine, you will reference the *name* of the Routine, *mark* the room for that part of the Routine, *front-* and *back-link* the steps in the Routine, and note *completion* of each Cluster of the Routine. Let's take a look!

Here is the formula we are going to use:

1. **Name the Transition. ("This MORNING...)**

2. **For each Cluster, mark the room we are in each time we change rooms. ("...while we are in the BATHROOM...")**

3. **Use the words: FIRST – THEN – NEXT to "front-linking" the order of the steps. ("FIRST you'll use the toilet, THEN I want you to wash your face, and NEXT you will brush your teeth.")**

4. **Use the words: NOW THAT WE and recap the steps they just did. ("Now that you used the toilet, washed your face, and brushed your teeth...."). I call this "back-linking."**

5. **Use the words: FINISH UP and ALL DONE to indicate completion. ("...let's FINISH UP in the bathroom by wiping the sink and then we'll be ALL DONE in here.")**

6. **Repeat Steps 1-5 for** each Cluster within the Routine

Fill in this formula for the Morning Routine.

When your kids come home after school, follow the same formula for their Afternoon Routine, but begin to also "Sprinkle" in the benefits. An example that adds Sprinkling to the formula might sound like this:

> *"Since it's AFTERNOON [Naming the Transition] and you're just coming in from the outside, FIRST [Front-linking] I'd like you to take your sneakers off. This is going to help keep our home cleaner [Sprinkling]."*

Repeat the formula, with Sprinkling, for their Evening Routine and introduce the Tomorrow Box! When you get to the last Cluster of the Evening Routine, which should place you in their bedroom, you can say something like:

> *"I got this basket for you. I think it will make it easier for you to carry your stuff from the front door to your bedroom. FIRST, let's put your book bag with your homework in the box so it's ready for you tomorrow morning. NEXT we'll pack up what you need for afterschool and THEN we'll pack up the clothes you'll wear tomorrow — then everything you need for tomorrow will be all ready for you in this box."*

What do you think? Experience tells me some of you are thinking something along the lines of, "That is so much better than nagging and yelling. I can't wait to get started." But there are also some of you who are thinking, "Who has time for all of that talking about what we're doing?" Or, "My kids will think I've been abducted by an alien if I start micro-managing them like that." But before you make up your mind one way or the other, let me just share these thoughts with you:

- It *is* a lot nicer than nagging and yelling and it works a lot better, too.
- If you don't think you have time to follow your kids around like that, let me ask you this: How much time do you spend backtracking, looking for misplaced items, and checking on them to see if they are doing what they are supposed to be doing, or coming along behind them to do it for them? Exactly! I know for a fact that doing it this way takes less time than any or all those other things.
- You'll only be in this phase for a very short time. Thanks to my *Signature Formula*, the back-linking and front-linking will help your kids internalize their sequences very quickly and you won't have to do or say ANYTHING to them!
- Okay, so maybe your kids *will* think something is 'up.' Do your best to be as casual as possible when you are sprinkling in the benefits….and remember, the new Routines will be making things much calmer at home and nicer for them, so they're going to want to do them!

Permission to Skip: Take What You Need and Skip the Rest

PRO TIP FOR OLDER CHILDREN: I will agree, however, that older children may be a bit resentful of your sudden 'over interest' in when and how they do these things. They also (I'd hope) don't require as much supervision and reminding. For that reason, you may need to take it down a notch for older kids. But please don't dismiss the need for Routines for older children because they're more independent than little ones. Routines make things flow better *for* everyone, and they instill a stronger sense of personal responsibility in your older kids.

PRO TIP FOR LITTLE ONES: On the flip side, toddlers and preschoolers may need even more detailed instructions. They do better with short, simple, one-step-at-a-time directions. Plus, you'll likely need to take more than two days to introduce the Routines by breaking them down even further. (But oh, the payoff!)

Day 9 Assignment:

- Read over the six-step formula for taking your kids through their Routines. Maybe write out a script with the specific details of your Routines.

- Rehearse what you're going to say, as well. You can just do this in your head or – even better – in front of a mirror. But I encourage you to practice what you will say so that it sounds natural – like how Mom always sounds (only maybe slightly more composed!).

- Roll out the Routines and introduce The Tomorrow Box, according to your script!

- Get excited about our second day of Rolling out Routines tomorrow!

Just another reminder before we get to the second day of introducing Routines to your kids. If you're feeling like you could use more detailed direction and guidance in making The *28-Day Stress-Free Family System* work its wonders for your family, feel free to visit my www.TheStressFreeFamily.com/go to find out more about The Stress-Free Family System Home Learning Program. This enhanced program comes with in-depth videos, in which I give additional examples and more detailed instructions as well as a comprehensive workbook with worksheets, templates, and checklists for all your planning and implementing. I also provide the complete scripts and model the whole thing for you from beginning to end including the what, why, how and examples!

Day 10:
Pillar 1 Routines – Step 6: Communicate (Part 2 of 2)

Today's Overview
- *Signature Moves*
  - Tomorrow Box (its first full day!)
  - Cementing the use of the Routines and Tomorrow Boxes
  - "Sprinkling" in benefits
- What you'll need
  - Tomorrow Boxes
  - Routines Checklists (in sheet protectors)
  - Dry erase markers

"A huge amount of success in life comes from learning as a child how to make good habits. It's good to help kids understand that when they do certain things habitually, they're reinforcing patterns."

~Charles Duhigg, American journalist

How did the first day of new Routines go with your kids? I'm betting that it went more smoothly than you might have anticipated. But if it didn't go perfectly, don't worry! We're going to be reinforcing what you rolled out yesterday by repeating, almost exactly, your scripts from yesterday. And just to be clear, you will not have to "script" every day with your children until they move out of the house! One of the beautiful things about this system is that a lot of work goes into the preparation and the precise implementation of the System. Getting it right the first time means that we get to quickly *dial back* all of those efforts, as things start moving along seamlessly. Plus, if your family experiences any backtracking in the weeks and months to come, you are already armed with the information you need to get everyone back on track – and fast!

Yesterday, we introduced the Tomorrow Box and left off with the script for the first day's Evening Routine. Therefore, TODAY is the first, FULL day of implementing their Routines WITH the Tomorrow Box.

In the morning, you will repeat what you did yesterday, walking them through the Morning Routine according to the formula and your script – and NOT telling them that it's their new "Routine"! The difference this morning is that when it's time to get dressed, your kids will be putting on the clothes that they have picked out and added to their Tomorrow Boxes. This means you get to talk about that and *Sprinkle* in the benefits of both picking out their clothing the night before and having everything at-the-ready in their Tomorrow Boxes!

Today's *Signature Move* is about cementing the use of the Tomorrow Box and how it works with their Routines, including how handy and helpful it is to them. You already know the elements that need to be included in your explanations (naming, marking, Front- and Back-Linking, indicating completion), but I'm going to further help you by walking you through the cementing today! This will help your understanding of how to use Sprinkling and the formula in combination to further your agenda. Ready to get started?

For your Routines today, you are going to go through the exact same process as you did yesterday. Using the formula, you will:

- Name the transition and the room
- Link the steps using the words *first, next, and then*.
- Complete by using the words *finish up* and all *done* to mark the end of Transitions.

What you're going to do differently today, is reinforce how well this is working by using more of my *Signature Move* by *Sprinkling* in the benefits throughout the day.

For example, you could say:

"Isn't it nice that all your clothes are right here in this box? We don't have to waste any time thinking about to wear or what we need. This is so easy. And your soccer uniform is all together in this drawstring bag with your cleats. I'm so happy we don't have to look for anything."

And when they're leaving for school, you might say something like:

"Since there's nothing left in the box, I guess that means you have everything with you that you need for the day! Great job! I'm going to leave this box right here at the door for you, so when you come home, you can just put your stuff in there."

SPRINKLING, SPRINKLING, SPRINKLING!

Can you imagine how great it's going to feel for you AND your child, knowing that they have everything they need to be successful for the day? No wasted time wondering, no anxiety over items left behind, and you won't be waiting for your child to call you to bring something they've forgotten! SUCCESS!

Remember: Once the Routines are established and become second-nature to everyone in the house, you won't have to follow them around saying these things. They will do them without having to be told. They will be ROUTINE.

<u>Day 10 Assignment</u>:

- Read over your scripts again, make any necessary changes, and ensure you have them down pat.
- Use your scripts to cement the Routines and the addition of the Tomorrow Box – Sprinkle, Sprinkle, Sprinkle.
- Celebrate your success!

Day 11:
Pillar 1 Routines – Steps 7 & 8:
Support with Reminders

and Practice Makes Progress

Today's Overview:
- *Signature Move*
  - o   Maintenance process for Routines
- You'll need
  - o   The same materials as on Day 10 (Tomorrow Boxes, Routines Checklists, dry erase markers)

"Over time, as the daily routines become second nature, discipline morphs into habit."

~Twyla Tharp, American dancer, choreographer, and author

Okay! Let's wrap up Routines so that we can move on to Pillar 2: Rhythms. (I literally cannot wait to tell you about Rhythms – you're going to love them!)

Today, we are going to discuss the final *two* steps for creating Routines, as they go hand-in-hand. Plus, the need for these last two steps doesn't just apply to today. Our steps "Supporting with Reminders" and "Practice Makes Progress" are your maintenance steps for your Routines. They keep you and your kids on track. Right now, your kids' Routines are still new and fresh, both to them and to you. Invest a little more time now to reinforce them, and a little time on an ongoing basis to encourage them, and you'll barely have to think about them anymore! Of course, you will always want to celebrate with your family how smoothly you're able to run your home. And Routines will need to be updated as your children grow up and take on new responsibilities. But in the meantime, you're not going to believe how easy it will become to accomplish all those have-to-dos that you used to struggle with. And when it's time to change your child's Routine, you and they now have the tools to make that revision easily!

To Support with Reminders, you'll approach today like you did the last two days, only go "script-lite" as you prompt your kids to complete their Routines. Allow them to complete their Routines on their own, only offering reminders – snippets of the full script – as they may need them.

That is, make simpler statements that still spell out what needs to happen, but you don't have to use the entire formula. You won't have to name the Transition, name the room or use all of the linking words. For example, you can simply state:

"When you come in the house, I'd like you to take off your shoes and bring your sweatshirt and bookbag into the kitchen, where we'll have our snack and do your homework."

With smaller kiddos, you can still use a statement like the one above, but you may need to change the language slightly to explain it on their level. And you may also need to continue to follow them through these steps – but they are going to become more and more independent with their Routines every day!

In order to begin to take you out of the process entirely, you're also going to give them the printed Routines checklists for the day. You're *still* not going to call them Routines, and you're going to keep it as low-key as possible. Simply say something like:

"I made you this list to make it easier for you to remember what you need to do every day. From now on, just cross off each step when you finish it with this special marker I got you. This will help you make sure you don't forget to do anything, and it will stay in your Tomorrow Box with this eraser."

Again, don't tell them anything else. You just made them a list. That's all!

You will continue to approach the kids' Routines like this each day (I'm going to remind you through the rest of the days to help keep you on track!), slowly backing off your prompts and reminders until they can complete the Routines as independently as possible. Obviously, older kids will be on their way to complete independence pretty quickly. Smaller children will continue to need more guidance. But again, it's going to be less and less over time. Just keep an eye on everyone, noticing when they are or are not anticipating their next steps. If they're forgetting something, just remember to use the same KEY words and give them a little nudge like:

"Remember, FIRST you wash your hands and THEN you brush your teeth, right?"

So, let's recap the rollout of Routines over the last three days. It will help you with this maintenance step in the days ahead:

1. **FOLLOW** your scripts for days 1 and 2.

2. **WATCH** to see when they begin anticipating the next step. Once that happens…

3. **SHOW** them the Routines checklist in the way that I described and instruct them to cross off each task as they finish. As they are nearing the completion of each Transition…

4. **REVIEW** the checklist with them to make sure they have crossed everything off.

That pretty much takes care of the first Pillar of the Stress-Free Family System! The last step in Routines is: Practice Makes Progress! Don't get upset if you think it's taking too long to "gel" with your kids. Just stick with it! And be sure to pat yourself on the back with every success, as well as to give your kids lots of smiles and high-fives for their successes!

We have already covered a lot and you're moving closer to your Stress-Free Family. You're going to begin to see some positive changes very quickly. But the real transformation comes after we sit your family down when we get to REVOLUTIONIZE. Right now, your family has no idea that this is the beginning of a Revolution because you are easing them into Routines slowly and *Sprinkling* in how great it all is and how much sense it all makes. But *you* know that every day, we are moving closer and closer to creating your Stress-Free Family! In the next chapter, we'll be introducing Rhythms, the second Pillar in The System. Rhythms are all about removing all the little speed bumps or hiccups that show up regularly and threaten to derail your day. Once you've gotten your Routines on autopilot, you don't want anything to get in the way of your Stress-Free day, right? Rhythms will take care of that.

It's time to get excited about Rhythms. They're everyone's favorite!

Day 11 Assignment:
- CONTINUE to guide your kids through their Routines with "script-lite" language.
- WATCH to see when they begin anticipating their next step.
- SHOW them the Routines checklist in the way that I described and instruct them to cross off each task as they finish.
- REVIEW the checklist with them to make sure they have crossed everything off.

Day 12:
Pillar 2 Rhythms – Getting Acquainted With The "Secret Sauce" of
RHYTHMS

Today's Overview

- *Signature Move*
  - o Identifying and resolving "speedbumps" or "hiccups" in our days
  - o Adding Rhythms to make your days effortless
- What you'll need
  - o Your journal for today's assignment
  - o Materials to keep your Routines on track as we add the remaining Pillars

---

"When the music changes, so does the dance."

~African proverb

Congratulations, Mama! You have "graduated" from Routines, Pillar 1 of The Stress-Free Family System! You've begun to change the "music" in your home by creating structure around your family's Transitions, and your kids are learning their "dance" steps. Next, I get to introduce you to everyone's favorite Pillar – a *Signature Move* and my *secret sauce* – Rhythms. This is where everyone's steps really begin to get in sync!

What are Rhythms?

Well, it helps to first recall how we defined Routines. A Routine is a step-by-step process that defines what, how, and when tasks are to be completed. But Routines apply to *a single person*. That is, YOU have your morning Routine, which consists of all the things YOU do to get up, get ready, and get out of the house. And your children have THEIR Routines of all the things THEY do to get up, get ready, and get out of the house. (If your kids are very small, you are helping them with the steps in their Routine, but the steps are still theirs, preparing THEM for their day.)

On the other hand, Rhythms are step-by-step processes that define what, how, and when tasks are to be completed *where two (or more) people* play a role in the process (you AND your child).

If Routines are what make your day easier, Rhythms are what will make your day effortless!

Rhythms are the solutions to challenges that can show up in your day, tripping you up and causing chaos. As I mentioned earlier, they're designed to address any "speed bumps" or "hiccups" we encounter on any given day. What makes the Rhythm work is that once you have identified the process, it is repeatable and sustainable. In other words, Rhythms make the problem GO AWAY.

Why do we need Rhythms in addition to Routines? Because even when a home has established Routines that are working (and working *well*), when we hit that speedbump again, chaos and stress continue in our homes. The *Signature Move* is that we identify and eliminate those speedbumps, once and for all, by creating a Rhythm.

To help you understand what this looks like I want to give you an example of a time where everyone in my family was marching to the beat of their own drum. Tomorrow, I'll show you how I created a Rhythm which eliminated the chaos of it all.

At the time, my boys were attending three different schools. They would come home with tons of notes and permission slips that needed to be signed, read, dealt with, and entered into the calendar. Often, that paperwork came home without the name of the school on it. With three different schools, I wouldn't even know which paper belonged to each kid! They would just dump the paperwork on my desk, the kitchen table, or even my nightstand. Occasionally, they'd hand me something directly, telling me it needed to be signed. Giving it to me directly would seem like the most effective way to ensure I got it, but I'd typically be in the middle of some other task, like making dinner, unable to deal with it immediately. Because I was busy, I'd set it aside for later, but then forget where I put it. Or worse, forget I'd been given it completely! Our chaotic non-process resulted in many lost or late permission slips, donations, and notes needing to be returned to the teacher.

Because the notes were always late and lost, my youngest son became very anxious and nervous and worried he'd miss out on a school trip or get in trouble for not bringing his notes back on time. Every time he got a note from school, he would follow me around asking me every two minutes to take care of it. I'm not exaggerating for effect here! He was the biggest pest in the world. My husband and I nicknamed him "relentless", which is actually a GREAT and very useful quality overall – just not in this particular context, if you know what I mean. He wanted me to immediately drop whatever I was doing and take care of his school notes, which, of course, I wasn't always able to do. I'd keep telling him I'd do it *later*, and he just kept badgering me! I just knew something had to give!

This situation presented two problems that needed to be solved:

- The notes were being lost and handed in late or not at all.
- These missing notes were causing stress and chaos at home—especially in the heart and mind of one of my children.

It was obvious that this situation was upsetting my youngest son. It was also annoying for me to have him asking me non-stop to sign something. I had to find a solution that would make us both happy.

To do that, I thought about what I didn't like about the situation and about some possible actions I could take to make the situation better and alleviate the stress and anxiety it was causing. I came up with a solution that worked for me and all three kids, and I'm going to tell you about how that Rhythm works in tomorrow. In fact, I'm going to share with you the three, key Rhythms we use in my house. (They are *Signature Moves* with my *Signature Move!*). Almost everyone who goes through The 28-Day Stress-Free Family System adopts these three Rhythms, as they take care of very common problems. After my three *Signature Move* Rhythms, I'm going to walk you through how to create a Rhythm of your own, so you'll know how to create one for any situation that trips your family up.

But let's get back to talking about Rhythms in general. A Rhythm, like a Routine, is the actual process that takes place, with clear-cut expectations and responsibilities for both parties. Each person knows what they are responsible for in the process. This clarity around who needs to do what and when is what helps keep us on track. Can you see how both you and your child need to work as a team to make certain problems in your home go away?

Anything that derails you from a smooth day requires a Rhythm. Again, I'm going to teach you three Rhythms that you can use or modify to greatly reduce disruptions and confusion in your home. But I also want you to be prepared to come up with Rhythms for anything *else* in *your* household that you want to smooth out. So, for today, I just want you to begin to think about what your family's particular "speedbumps" are. You'll have some time to think it over as you get acquainted with my three *signature* Rhythms, and then we'll get to work on additional Rhythms your family needs!

Day 12 Assignment:

- Routines!
  - o Continue to Support with Reminders.
  - o Don't forget: Practice Makes Progress!
- Take a few minutes to think about the situations in your household that disrupt the flow and/or cause anxiety in one or more members of your family. Jot your thoughts down in your journal.
  - o What distracts you from what you need to do?
  - o What could go more smoothly?
  - o What is causing stress for you or your kids?
  - o You just identified your family's "pain points," as they are inflicting pain on one or more members of your family. You'll be creating Rhythms for these pain points.
- If you didn't come up with anything, it's possible that you just can't think of these disruptions and annoyances because you're so used to them that you don't give them much thought. They've become a "given" in your life so they don't automatically pop up on your radar. Reading about my signature Rhythms will likely help you recognize a few of your own pain point. Give it a few days and see what you notice!
- Begin to think about how you might resolve your home's hiccups. As I walk you through my three *Signature Move* Rhythms over the next few days, it should help you come up with ideas for your specific pain points. And on Day 16, I'll take you through the step-by-step process for creating a Rhythm.

Day 13:
Pilar 2 Rhythms – *Signature* Notes Folder

Today's Overview

- *Signature Moves*
  - o Eliminate chaos over kids' paperwork with Notes Folder Rhythm
  - o Color coding
- What you'll need
  - o Your journal
  - o Large, clear plastic folder or envelope for each child

"When mama ain't happy, ain't nobody happy."

~ Songwriters, Tim Nichols, Richard C. Giles, Gilles Godard

That lyric, from a country music song, can now be found on coffee mugs, plaques, and t-shirts, and do you know why? Because it's true, right? As the CEO of your home, you set the tone for everyone in it. And as the choreographer of the "*Rhythm*" of the home, you need to be able to plan the steps so that everyone follows along in sync – instead of stepping on each other's toes.

Let's think about Rhythms as a means to help mama stay happy. Moms who have gone through The 28-Day Stress-Free Family training tell me that this is their favorite Pillar!

Remember my troubles keeping track of school notes for three boys in three schools and the anxiety it was causing one of them? I considered what was currently happening, what the problems were, and how we might handle school notes differently. The solution I put together is simply called my Notes Folder Rhythm.

After analyzing the problem, I decided to give each of my children a big zippered plastic folder. I put a sticker with their name on it and stuck to my color coding, so we could easily identify which Notes Folder belonged to whom. I told them that from that moment on, anything that came home from school that I needed to deal with should be placed in the Notes Folder and on the kitchen counter when they get home from school.

I made this small but important task part of their Afternoon Routine. That's the beginning of *their* part of the Rhythm.

Here's where my part begins. And I have a few different *moves* on my part, depending on what turns up in the folder. As part of my Routine, I look at the Notes Folders early in the evening and handle any notes from the school appropriately:

- If there's a note in the Notes Folder that's general information from the school, I read it and save or dispose of it, accordingly.

- If the Notes Folder contains something I simply need to review and sign, I review and sign it, and return it to the folder.

- If what appears in the Notes Folder is an item I need to talk to them about, or if I have a question about something, I *leave it on top* of the Notes Folder on the kitchen counter and it becomes something we discuss during breakfast.
   o After we talk about it at breakfast, I deal with what needs to be done with the paperwork and it goes back into the Notes Folder.

- If I have anything I need to send to school (e.g., a note to the school nurse), it also goes into the Notes Folder and is then put in their book bag.

Then I put the Notes Folders into their book bags, which lets them know that my part is done.

After I have handled papers and placed Notes Folders into their book bags, the Rhythm – our little dance – goes back to them for the final step in the dance. That is, notes get back to school and get there on time. When they get to school, the presence of the Note Folder in their bag alerts them to the need to return something to their teacher or someone else at school!

See how this Rhythm takes the pain out of school notes by clarifying what my kids' responsibilities are and what my responsibilities are, as well as *when* we will handle those responsibilities? My children and I always know where the notes are. My kids know that if they have something they want or need me to look at, it must be in the Notes Folder and on the kitchen counter for me to deal with it. Once it's on the kitchen counter, it becomes my responsibility. I will deal with papers by the morning and make it my responsibility to either put it back into their book bag at night OR discuss it with them in the morning. Adding this process to our life keeps our house *in Rhythm*. I'm not searching through my desk or on my nightstand for paperwork they dumped because I know it's in the Notes Folder on the kitchen counter. I'm not chasing them down trying to figure out which note belongs to which child because each child has their notes in their own Notes Folder. And once it is in their folder, it becomes their responsibility. It also alleviates the anxiety because they know it will be taken care of and they always know that the notes are either in their backpack in the Notes Folder or on the kitchen counter in the Notes folder.

If your child goes to school, you are either currently or *will* be buried in papers from school. Can you see how this simple, repeatable *Rhythm* can simplify the process – and make your life so much easier?

As I mentioned, I use transparent, color-coded, plastic zippered folders/envelopes for my boys' Notes Folders. The colors let me know whose is whose at a glance, and I can quickly see if they are empty or full because they're transparent. I highly recommend getting this type of zippered plastic folder as it is heavier duty than regular paper folders and will be able to withstand the back and forth. The zipper also makes sure nothing falls out. Lastly, I suggest that the zippered plastic folders be larger than 8 ½ x 11 so that all of their paperwork or folders fit neatly inside. You can get these anywhere you can get school or office supplies.

Now let's move on how to introduce the Notes Folder to your children. When your kids come home from school, show them where the Notes Folders are waiting for them. Say something like what follows:

From now on, every time your teacher gives you a note, put it into your new Notes Folder. As soon as you get home from school, every day, put your Notes Folder, in this tray. This tray will always be here on the corner of the counter. After you put the Notes Folder in the tray, it will be my job to look through the notes and put it back in your folder. If I need to discuss something with you about the Notes, we'll do it at breakfast and then your Notes Folder will go right into your backpack. So, from now on, you won't need to ask me about it anymore or be worried that your notes will be lost or late. From now on they will be in your Notes Folder either in your backpack or this tray right here on the counter. Sound good?

And when you get to school in the morning, all you have to do is give your teacher the notes that are in the Notes Folder. Any questions? Great.

Then ask them:

So, what happens if your teacher gives you a note tomorrow morning? What will you do when you get home from school tomorrow? Do you know what will happen next? What if I have a question about the notes, or want to discuss it with you? Then what happens? What will you do when you get to school? Any questions?

I'm excited to start this tomorrow morning so we won't have to worry about lost or late notes anymore.

I've found that some parents prefer to go over their children's notes after school or at dinner, if that's you, just tweak my example. Just tell them to leave the Notes Folder on the kitchen counter and you'll review it and discuss it with them after dinner—whatever works for you. The idea is that any notes they bring home from school and any note that goes from you to the school goes in the folder.

<u>Day 13 Assignment:</u>

- Routines!
    - o Continue to Support with Reminders.
    - o Don't forget: Practice Makes Progress.
- Buy or find something to work as Notes Folders for each of your children.
- Introduce the Notes Folders Rhythm to them when they get home from school.

Day 14:
Pillar 2 Rhythms – *Signature* Prime Time Rhythm

Today's Overview

- *Signature Move*
  - o Get out of the house on time with the Prime Time Rhythm
- What you'll need
  - o A clock or timer

"If you have children, the demands made upon you during the first hour of the morning can make the job of an air traffic controller seem like a walk in the park."

~ J. Wurtman

My second *Signature* Rhythm emerged from the pain point of leaving the house late all the time. Almost daily, I'd be frantically trying to finish getting ready, trying to leave on time, and my children would start talking about something or doing something that would distract me. They'd ask me for a playdate after school or start playing with a toy or begin pulling things out of their drawer. I'd be trying to get my children out the door and off to school on time and whatever they were asking me for didn't need to be handled at that exact moment. It was distracting and disrupting the flow of what they needed to do AND disrupting what I needed to do.

We relieved this pain point by instituting a Rhythm we call "Prime Time." The Prime Time Rhythm refers to the 10 minutes prior to when we need to leave the house for any reason. Prime Time means we do and say *only* things that move us toward our departure. That is, we only talk about or do things that move us closer to the goal of getting out the door on time, successfully and calmly. And because it can be so frustrating to do anything but the essentials during these 10 minutes, there are consequences for doing or saying anything else. For example, if I'm asked about a weekend playdate during Prime Time, that would be an example of a non-essential question. Because a weekend playdate has nothing to do with getting us out of the door on time, right? So, in my home, the answer to a non-essential question asked during Prime Time is an automatic and clear "No." Why? Because during Prime Time, I don't have time to think about the logistics of the weekend playdate. I only have time to do or say things that move us toward our goal of leaving the house on time calmly and with everything we need.

During Prime Time, the answer to any nonessential question will always be a resounding "No." That's a relevant consequence. Once I explained Prime Time to them, it didn't take long for them to understand that it wasn't worth it to ask a non-essential question during those 10 minutes.

If during Prime Time, I heard them talking or doing something non-essential, I asked them if it was moving us toward our goal. That little cue clarified that it was Prime Time and also helped them to learn what was and was not essential.

Some of you might wonder why I would limit what my children could talk to me about and when. The answer: I need those 10 minutes before we leave our home to be free from disruption. (And believe me, so do you!) It's when we need to focus on wrapping up our Morning Routines and clarifying what's to happen after school, who will be picking them up, and so forth.

Wouldn't having Prime Time help you move through your day more effortlessly? If so, include "Prime Time" as one of your Rhythms. If you need some help with the language for introducing Prime Time to your kids, here's a brief script.

> *"I've been thinking about this morning and how we got to school late…again. I want us both to have a calm morning tomorrow morning. Don't you? So, can you think of something we can do to make it easier?"*

See what they come up with, you might be surprised! They may even help you create some new Rhythms. After listening to them, give them the Prime Time idea by using this script as an example.

> *"It's hard for me to focus on everything I have to do to get out on time when I'm distracted by questions that don't have to do with us getting to school on time. So tomorrow, ten minutes before we leave, we're going to start what I'm going to call 'Prime Time.' I'll say, "Prime Time," and we will all know that from that point on until we leave for school, we can only talk about or do things that help us get out the door on time.*

> *"If you start talking to me about something that doesn't have to do with getting us out of the door on time, I'm going to say, "Prime Time," And that way you'll know that we need to talk about that later. Got it?"*

Day 14 Assignment:
- Routines!
  - o Continue to Support with Reminders.
  - o Don't forget: Practice Makes Progress.

- Notes Folder:
    - o How's it going? If you're still being handed notes or finding them in odd places, just redirect your kids to the Notes Folder. Soon they will be adding their school papers to the folder without prompting!
- This evening or tomorrow morning, explain "Prime Time" to your kids.
    - o Clarify that it applies before leaving for school every day, as well as for any other time you're headed out of the house.
    - o Give them examples of essential and non-essential things that could be said or done during Prime Time.
    - o Be clear that any questions asked during Prime Time result in the answer of "No."

Day 15:
Pillar 2 Rhythms – *Signature* Dinner Conversation Rhythm

Today's Overview

- *Signature Move*
    - o Keep questions and other chaos to a minimum Dinner Conversation Rhythm
- PRO TIPS
- What you'll need
    - o Dry erase whiteboard and marker for my PRO TIP, sharing information over dinner. [Optional]

"Effective performance is preceded by painstaking preparation."

~ Brian Tracy, American self-development speaker and author

As I did on Day 14, I'm going to begin sharing the Dinner Conversation Rhythm by describing the pain point that gave birth to this Rhythm. I'm pretty confident that you deal with this pain point in your house, as well. How much time is dedicated to hearing kids ask you the same question over and over again and telling them the same thing over and over again?

- What's for dinner?
- What's for lunch?

- What am I doing after school tomorrow?
- Who's picking me up?

In my house, it would be the same questions – from all three kids! – several times a day, every day. It was too much! To stop the madness, I added "Dinner Conversation" to our Rhythms. Every night at dinner, I take a few minutes each night to go over three things:

1. What we're eating.
2. What's happening after school tomorrow.
3. What's happening this evening.

These three items are pretty much all-inclusive when it comes to the questions children have—the ones asked repeatedly. Creating a Rhythm to address all three topics, when we all have time to talk about them, ensures that:

- Everyone is informed.
- Curiosities are satisfied.
- A sense of calm prevails.

See how this Rhythm clearly defines our responsibilities? The kids know what information I will be sharing with them and when.

Again, I'd like to help you with some specific wording that I know has been effective for all the moms I've worked with over the last 10 years.

PRO TIP: This is when you will want to use a small tabletop dry erase board. Start with the morning, when they wake up, and fill in the details – what you're eating, what's happening today, what to expect for tomorrow. If your child cannot read yet, draw symbols or little pictures to help them understand what's on the board. You might also consider getting a magnetic board and use laminated stickers with magnets attached to the back of them or a felt board and use felt pieces.

PRO TIP: For meals, as with everything, offer them no more than two options. It's much harder to make a decision when we are given many options. Make it easier on them – and yourself – by limiting the options to two!

As you are writing these things down, read it aloud, so that everyone understands what is going on and is in agreement. When you are done writing, say:

"See how I wrote down everything we agreed to for tomorrow? Now we all know what's for breakfast, lunch, and dinner. We're also clear on what's going on after school, so now you don't have to wonder about it. I'm going to leave this board right here on the kitchen table, so whenever you forget or need a reminder, you'll have it. And it will be here in the morning before you go to school, so you can have one more look at how the day is going to play out before we head out the door."

PRO TIP: This one is CRITICAL. *Always* explain *how* your new ways of doing things will benefit *everyone* involved. Also, it's important to be consistent with your Rhythms – along with *all* the Pillars in this system. Consistency is one of the major elements of success to this system. If you aren't consistent it won't work. Remember: *The 28 Day Stress-Free Family System* is a *system* that works when you take it one step at a time and integrate all five Pillars. With the addition and integration of each new Pillar, your house will grow increasingly less chaotic and increasingly more calm and harmonious.

<u>Day 15 Assignment:</u>

- Routines – Practice Makes Progress.

- Notes Folder Rhythm – Check and prompt, as needed. Don't forget to *Sprinkle!*

- Prime Time Rhythm – How's it going? Have you had to give an automatic "no," yet? If so, don't worry! It only takes one or two before they learn to stick with essentials during Prime Time!

- Introduce Dinner Conversation Rhythm.

  o If your kids start with the questions, tell them you will share with them everything they need to know over dinner.

  o At the dinner table, explain that every night at dinner, you will inform them about upcoming meals, plans for tonight and tomorrow, as well as any other topic they tend to bombard you with questions about.

Day 16:
Pillar 2 Rhythms - Get into the Rhythm – How to Create Your Own

Today's Overview
- *Signature Move*
  - o This one's for YOU! What will be <u>your</u> Signature Rhythm?
- PRO TIPS
- What you'll need
  - o Your journal
  - o Any supplies you determine you will need to implement your new Rhythm

---

Life's problems wouldn't be called "hurdles" if there wasn't a way to get over them.

~Author Unknown

Sometimes we tolerate frustrations, thinking they're just a part of life. And of course, we can't control everything that happens to us. However, in most situations, we can exert some control over the outcome. We may not be able to eliminate every pain point, but we can often minimize the amount of pain we have to experience.

We have already covered – and I hope you have implemented – some version of my three *signature Rhythms* that all my Stress-Free moms love. Those three alone will massively reduce the amount of chaos in your home. But I want to equip you with a process for creating your very *own* signature Rhythm so that you can tailor what you're learning to *your* family.

Before we get started, I'm going to share the story of how my fabulous book editor, Melissa Lehman, who started implementing The Stress-Free Family System as soon as she started reading my manuscript, created her own signature Rhythm to smooth out afternoons.

Like many parents these days, Melissa drives her two energetic and talkative girls, Emily and Cora, to and from school. Because The 28-Day Stress-Free Family System helped Melissa get a lock on the family's Morning and Afterschool Routines, the rides to school happened seamlessly and getting into the house after school was also a breeze. However, the short drive home from the school – minutes that felt like hours – was the most stressful and frustrating part of Melissa's day. Allow me to set the scene.

Melissa would arrive at the schools, excited to see her girls' smiling faces at the end of the day. Typically, the girls would climb into the car with big smiles, but then things would go south. Fast. One of two things would happen. The first was requests to go *straight* to a store to buy something. The girls would have seen a friend with something they just *had* to have right away– shoes, jewelry, hair ties, you name it. Emily would want to go to Target for new headbands, and Cora would want to go to the shoe store for new boots, "just like Sophie's." Occasionally, the girls actually really needed something, like a new lunchbox because the current one was starting to fall apart. But even these things could wait for a planned visit to the store. But not to the girls! They expected Mom to handle all requests IMMEDIATELY.

In addition to the fact that Melissa doesn't buy her kids everything they demand, Melissa was very time-crunched after school, needing to hurry home to make dinner and take care of other responsibilities. She definitely did *not* have time to drive to the store *right now*. But even though she didn't have the time to do it, she'd sometimes give in – because she didn't want to say "no" again and hear, "Why not?!" or "You're mean!"

PRO TIP: Inconsistency *always creates* chaos. Be consistent in all aspects of this system!

The second thing they'd do on the drive home is tell Melissa something about their day that they didn't like. Maybe a friend ditched Emily at lunch. Maybe the teacher yelled at Cora's group, but it was only the *boys* who were goofing off. (So unfair!) The problem wasn't the complaints. Melissa was glad that they wanted to share with her and that she could be someone to lean on. The problem was they'd go on and on about whatever was upsetting about the day, and no one offered anything good to say. Worse yet, the two girls would often end up bickering about whose day was worse! Talk about a contest you shouldn't want to win, right?

For the longest time, Melissa just braced herself every day for the car ride home, accepting this daily discord as part of their lives. But once she noticed how well my *Signature Rhythms* worked, she decided to combine the ideas of Prime Time and Dinner Conversation Rhythms to create "Fab Five and Drive." This is what her new Rhythm looks like:

- Mom gets the first five minutes of the drive. She asks each of them about their day and takes a few minutes to set up the expectation of how the rest of their day will go. This way, she doesn't feel bombarded as soon as they get in the car.

- Then each daughter gets 5 five minutes to report anything that happened to them during the day, both good and bad.

  o If they have a "bad story," they have to either follow it with a solution for next time or get it off their chests quickly. This way, they got the time they needed to gripe, but there were some parameters around it. Once it was spoken about, it was over and not be brought up again later!

- Each girl – including Mom! – shares something she is grateful for, so they end their drive on a good note.

- All requests to go somewhere other than home become an automatic "NO."
- All requests to buy anything nonessential are an automatic "NO."
- Requests to buy essential items come with a reminder to hold all needs until they get home when Mom can make a note. This way, Melissa has some time to *decide* which items she will buy and then plans can be made as to *when* to buy them. She even decided that she would start making Friday's a "treat day" and sometimes they would go for ice cream and sometimes they would go shopping!

Isn't that great? For one, Melissa's Rhythm gave them something to say when they got in the car that prevented them from jumping right into why today was a "bad" day. That is, she filled the time with something better. And she did allow them to share good and bad, but she put limits around it. Finally, she offered them something of value to fill in the time by sharing information about what's going on for the evening. It also took the pressure off of Melissa having to make an immediate decision about whether or not to buy the girls what they wanted. This way, she set the expectation for the girls, and the drive home became fabulous when each person had the floor for 5 minutes. That's how she came up with the name "Fab Five and Drive"!

And guess what? It worked immediately. I love how she put her own spin on it and made it work for her family!

Are you ready to start creating Rhythms that will help *your* family function better? Great! Here's the process.

Step 1: Identify the Problem

What are the speedbumps or hiccups derailing your day? What do you or your children do that throw a curve ball into your otherwise well-oiled Routines—you know, the Routines you just initiated in your home?

Take some time to think about this. It may be a small thing and it may only happen infrequently. Think about the situations that make you crazy. The ones that make you say, "I could really have done without that today." Or, "If you ask (do, say) that one more time...."

Step 2: Decide what needs to happen instead of what is happening now

This is your opportunity to dream about what you want your conversations and interactions with your family to be like. Write down what you *want* the situation to look like instead of the problem scenario. What do you *want* to happen?

Don't give up on your dream scenario, thinking "They'll never go along with that," or "Things never change." Your children will sync with you if you provide the structure. They've learned not to get up at school and walk over to talk to a friend during class. They've learned to follow the teacher's "Rules" for prescribed bathroom breaks. The teachers have provided the structure and they adhere to it. They'll learn to follow your lead, too!

But don't *over*estimate your children's abilities. You cannot expect a three-year-old to never get restless in the car. Neither can you expect an excited ten-year-old to stick with the Rhythm of not asking questions when she's excited to attend a birthday party this weekend. Be resolute, but gracious, too.

Step 3: Brainstorm possible solutions

What are some reasonable and viable things you can do to fix the problem—to add a *Rhythmic* flow to your Routine in order to keep everyone on track?

Write down a few possible solutions so you can really study them. You want to be able to think about each solution from a practical and logistical point of view. Writing them down allows you to better visualize the steps of each solution in your mind's eye.

Step 4: Determine the specific steps and responsibilities for your Rhythm

Okay, now that you have a few possible scenarios for putting a Rhythm into place to fix your problem, it's time for you to decide which scenario you want to use, along with the when, where, and how of it all.

The WHEN, WHERE, and HOW of your new Rhythm:

- <u>When</u>: What part of the day will be best for handling this situation? What part of the day will you be able to give the situation the time it deserves? What part of the day will your children be most receptive to what is going on *and* be able to retain the information being given to them?

- <u>Where</u>: The car? The dinner table? Bedtime? The breakfast table? Downtime spent together? Where will your children be able to best listen and not just hear? Where will you be able to handle the situation so that everyone is involved?

- <u>How</u>: What means of communication will work best? Talking? A chart they can refer to? A central drop-off point? The answer to this will depend on the nature of the situation you are trying to correct, the age of your children, and the desired outcome.

Step 5: Visualize successfully eliminating the pain point

This may sound like a repeat of what you've done in the last two steps. But this final step before you introduce the Rhythm to your family helps build your confidence about success. It also allows you one last mental walk-through to ensure that your approach is going to result in the improved outcome you seek. For example, during the visualization step, Melissa realized that she really wanted to reinforce the idea that the car ride home was going to be a positive uplifting time for her daughters, so she went back and added the gratitude piece so that the car rides would always end on a positive note.

Can you see how simple it is? Rhythms aren't complicated. They are simply consistent, pre-determined solutions that eliminate (or seriously minimize) the pain points. But boy do they work! And that's why Rhythms are moms' favorite Pillar of *The 28 Day Stress-Free Family System!*

Day 16 Assignment:

- Keep up with your Routines – Practice Makes Progress! Your Routines go more and more smoothly every day now, right?!

- Maintain Notes Folder, Prime Time, and Dinner Conversations Rhythms – Keep reinforcing and *Sprinkling!*

- Use the steps above to create your *own Signature* Rhythm of another pain point in your home.

Day 17:
Pillar 3 Rules – Introduction to
RULES

Today's Overview
- *Signature Moves*
  - o Rules Trifecta
  - o Rules for Mom
- What you'll need
  - o Your journal for today's assignment

"Discipline is wisdom and vice versa."

~M. Scott Peck American psychiatrist and best-selling author
of The Road Less Traveled

Welcome to the Third Pillar of *The 28-Day Stress-Free Family System*, Rules! Rules were bound to come up eventually, right? Notice the word "discipline" in the quote above. In that sentence, "discipline" refers to following prescribed behaviors or self-control. It does not pertain to the *enforcement* of behavior or "punishment," which is often the first thing that comes to mind when we hear "discipline." I point this out because The 28-Day Stress-Free Family System is about having *disciplined kids*, not having *to discipline your kids*! That is, when you have this system in place, when we add Rules and Rewards and put it all together to Revolutionize your home, your kids will be doing the things they're supposed to do and managing their own behaviors. You'll be eliminating the nagging, shouting, threats ("I'll throw all your toys away!), and punishments (actually taking toys away – temporarily!) – the day-to-day need *to discipline your kids*!

I'm dying to jump right into this Pillar and to show you how my approach is different than any Rules-based guidance you've seen in the past.   But before we get started, I have a confession to make.

I shared with you the story that represented the turning point in my parenting journey. (I'm sure you didn't forget, but here's a hint: It involved wearing two different shoes and a tearful conversation with my sister.) I knew something had to be done but creating structure in my home life wasn't something I really wanted to do. *Work* is structured. It's full of deadlines, Routines, and expectations (which is why it's called "work," I guess!). I wanted my *home* to be relaxed, easy, and FREE. I wanted to be the fun mom and just go with the flow. But I tried that, and it just doesn't work – for me or for my kids. The good news is that building the structure at home IS the thing that allows the feelings of freedom and ease we all want for our families! The structure is what ultimately "makes room for" the fun!

I already alluded to how *The 28-Day Stress-Free Family System* creates opportunities for fun in the first chapter on Routines. When your home is running smoothly, and your children are behaving, everyone has more time and energy to relax and enjoy one another. You're not putting out fires and making sure everyone has taken care of their responsibilities – because now they're clear on what those responsibilities are, as well as how to do those things effectively. They're not wasting time or asking you tons of questions, because they know what to expect for today. Things get accomplished calmly and efficiently. You should already be noticing some of these changes in your family, but it will continue to get better and better as we work through the rest of the Pillars.

In addition to our Routines and Rhythms, we need to have Rules to maintain our structure and our systems. In the Stress-free Family System, I encourage moms to use the word "expectations" because it has a more positive connotation than Rules. But I use Rules in during our training for clarity, because every mom knows exactly what I mean when I talk about creating Rules in the home. To further clarify, "Rule" is defined as "an authoritative principle set forth to guide behavior or action." And of course, in the home, parents are the authority setting forth the guidelines for everyone in the house.

Now that we have that defined, let's talk about my *Signature Move*, the Rules Trifecta! In my program, I recommend having three types of Rules: Rules for the kids, Rules for the home, and Rules for *Mom!*

Over the next two days, we'll spend a little bit of time on Rules for the kids and the home. But we're going to spend the bulk of our time in the Rules Pillar talking about Rules for Mom because this is a new concept for moms!

Rules for Mom

Before I explain why you need Rules for yourself, I just want to give you another friendly reminder that we are not sharing anything about Rules with the kids. And you won't be sharing the Rules for kids with them until day 28 when you have your family meeting. (Which, by the way, is going to make them feel like they made up their Rules themselves!). However, for the Rules you make for yourself today, you WILL be telling them "in the moment" what your Rule is, but you won't be telling them that it IS a Rule. I will make this clearer for you and give you real-world examples, too.

Here's the thing: Moms need Rules! Most parents know they need to have Rules for our kids, but we don't think about the need for Rules for ourselves. Parents need Rules, too! I'm going to ask you to shift the focus off of your kids and think about what you can expect from yourself. What Rules could you honor that would help you become the mom that you really want to be? Think about your pain points. Think about what drains your energy. Think about the dynamics between you and your kids that you'd like to change.

I talk a lot about energy and how important it is to safeguard and protect your energy. Parenting can zap your energy quick as lightning when things aren't running smoothly. When we're so busy giving, and giving, and being worn down, we can end up completely depleted and defeated at the end of any given day. I have met hundreds of moms who don't have any energy reserves at the end of the day for either themselves or their partner. How many moms do you know who don't even have the energy to *think* about that? Or worse yet, who've completely *forgotten* what it is that they actually like to do because it's been so long since they had the energy to think about it, much less plan anything? (Am I talking about *you* right now?) Do you have hobbies you still get to enjoy? Do you have creative outlets you do Routinely?

If your answers to those questions are "no" or "not nearly often enough," I want to help you change that for yourself. I want you to have more for yourself and more for your family. So, when I talk about Rules for yourself, I'm talking about you taking the power to change those energy-draining scenarios in your home. These are your pain points. (Remember, we started with pain points for Routines and Rhythms, too!) Think about them and write them down. We're going to flip those scenarios and stop all the energy leaks!

I encourage you to come up with Rules for yourself. Rules that are relevant and make sense to *you and allow you to be the best mom you can be.* My Rules for Mom were among the first parts of the system that I created, and I came up with a list of my "ten commandments." I will share a few of these with you – and you can adopt them if they're a good fit for you – but I really want you to come up with your own. This may seem strange at first, but I assure you that creating Rules for yourself creates sound boundaries around how you behave as a mom, as well as what you are and are not willing to tolerate as a mom.

So, I told you that when I set out on this journey I 'decided to decide.' One of the first things I decided was, **"Today, I will be playing the part of Mom."**

It seems obvious, right? We signed up for this, and it's the best job in the world. However, it's sometimes easy to forget that, even though we love it so much, that it *is* a *job*. And isn't it also the most important job in the world? Another reason we can accidentally step out of the role of Mom is that our kids can *forget* that we play the role of Mom. They want to make decisions that are really Mom's to make. They want you to *explain* why things should or should not be a certain way. Basically, they try to take over our job as Mom. As much as I encourage their participation in the home, and I am willing to consider their input and choices (when I ask), I ultimately realized that I am the mom, and it's my job to make the decisions. Therefore, I made myself a Rule around that. If you have similar experiences in your home, where your kids are bossing you around (or at least trying to), this could be a good Rule for you, too.

Another of my ten commandments is, **"A NO will not turn into a YES."** If your house is anything like mine was, I bet you can guess how I came up with this Mom Rule. My kids were wearing me down. They'd ask me for something, I'd tell them 'no,' and then they'd ask me, over and over again, until I was completely worn out, and I'd give in and say 'yes.' Not only was this annoying and energy-sucking, it left me feeling completely out of control.

Here's the thing: We *want* to say 'yes' to our kids as often as it's possible, responsible, and safe, right? But when you give a 'yes' that only came out of exhaustion and frustration over the repeated 'no's,' it doesn't feel good at all. You want to create situations where you think, "YAY! I get to say 'YES!' This will make my kids so happy, which makes me happy!" Otherwise, you feel resigned, defeated, and tired. And let's face it, how many times have you given in and then had negative feelings about your kids and yourself? Like, "I hope they enjoy it because they are *never* eating ice cream again!" You're mad at them and at yourself, right? I wanted to change this dynamic and change this pain point of being worn down and feeling defeated. And don't you, too? So, I asked myself, "What would make me happy?" "What would make me feel good about this?" "What would make me feel like I was doing a *good* job as a mom."

The answers were that I wanted to demonstrate that I have boundaries and am consistent. I wanted to teach them that when I *say* "no" I *mean* "no." I knew that doing that would teach them a valuable lesson and make me feel like I was doing great as their mom. I wanted to be able to say, "No," and simply hear, "Okay, Mom," in return. That would be an energy-gaining interaction for me, instead of an energy-draining one. The pain point of being worn down by repeated requests was turned around by this simple Rule for me.

The key was that I *committed* to this Rule. No matter how much they'd badger me, even if they asked me 50 times, I knew that my "no" wasn't turning into a "yes". So, the very next time they asked me for something and my answer was no, I was ready. When they asked me again, I simply told them – without saying that it was a Rule – that, from now on, a no would not turn into a yes, even if they asked me 50 times. Of course, at first, they tried to test to see if I would buckle. Because they'd learned from my past behavior that I could be worn down. Initially, they continued to ask for what they wanted over and over. It was still frustrating, but I knew that all I had to do was outlast them. And I also knew that afterward, I would get to continue to feel good about my mom skills because I stuck to my "no" and didn't give a "yes" from a place I knew I'd regret.

It didn't take long for this to change. Once I committed to this Rule, my kids learned very quickly that they could ask me 50, 100, or even 1,000 times, and they wouldn't get a different answer. They figured out it was a waste of time and learned to accept my answer and move on.

Of course, if you want to make this a Rule for yourself, you will have to decide for yourself whether or not this is one of the Rules you want to adopt for yourself. But I've never met a parent who did not need this Rule in their life!

I'm going to share a third of my Rules for Mom – another *commandment* – with an example. One of the moms I worked with had this "A-Ha!" moment while learning my system. It had to do with WHY her kids sometimes did the things she asked them to do and sometimes did not. Let me set the scene. Jessica's kids' playroom would be messy – toys beyond the ones they were playing with were spread out all over the place. Jessica knew from past experience that, "Clean up the playroom," was too broad an instruction for kids, so she'd break it down into specific steps. Thinking she was being pretty smart, she'd start with, "Could you put away the dolls?"

Can you guess what would happen next? Well, *sometimes*, one of them would start putting away the dolls. But, more often than not, they simply wouldn't do it, or they'd answer, "No, thank you." (At least they were polite, I guess!)

Another question for you: Did you notice what Jessica was doing wrong?

She was *asking* them to do something that she really should have been *telling* them to do. As soon as she adopted this Mom Rule: **"I will not ask a question when I'm giving a direction,"** her children started cleaning up every time she directed them! Do you do this yourself? Do you say things to your kids like, "Can you pick your jacket up off the floor?" That's a question. Think about how you "tell" your kids to do things (or start listening to yourself if you're not sure) and look for three clues that you're asking a question.

First, does it *sound* like a question? You know what I mean – with that little higher pitched lilt added in at the end of the sentence. Second, it ends in a question mark. That one should be obvious. Finally, the clue that's the "smoking gun" telling you it's a question is that it gives them the opportunity to answer "no." Guess what? If you give them an opening to say "no," odds are they are going to take it!

(It took some practice and a few slip-ups, but Jessica got used to giving directions instead of asking for tasks to be completed!)

And here's how to let your kids know about this Rule. Don't say anything about the Rule at all! Just stop *asking* and start *directing*. When you want your kids to do something, and you're not giving them a choice about it, don't give them a choice about it! Change every, "Can you pick your jacket up off the floor?" to "Sara, pick your jacket up off the floor and hang it up now." No question mark, no opportunity to answer the question with a no. And don't lilt it at the end *as if* it were a question, because it's not! Stop asking questions and start giving directions.

Now that I've given you examples of my Rules for Mom, the pain points they grew out of, and how to incorporate them into your life, it's your turn.

Day 17 Assignment:
- Routines!
  - o Your kids should be "getting it" by now. Continue to provide just enough support to keep them on track!
- Rhythms!
  - o Same as above!
- Rules!
  - o Think about the pain point scenarios in your home. Write them down along with a couple of words about how they make you *feel*.
  - o That's all you need to do for now. We'll develop and adopt Rules for Mom in the next chapter!

Day 18:
Pillar 3 Rules – Developing and Adopting Rules for Mom

Today's Overview
- *Signature Move*
  - o Declaring Rules for Mom
- What you'll need
  - o Your journal
  - o A mirror
  - o Your commitment

"Sometimes the strength of motherhood is greater than natural laws."

~Barbara Kingsolver, American novelist, essayist, and poet

That quote makes me think, "Yes, yes, YES!" How about you? Motherhood is *hard*, but we've been given the super-human strength that goes along with the role. I hope that you are finding that The 28-Day Stress-Free Family System is already reducing the stress and chaos in your home. I want to honor you for doing this *work* and to remind you that it's only *work* for a short time – you are getting so close to a calm, easy home! If you're feeling excited, GREAT! It's only going to get better. *Don't give up!* You're almost there! So, let's wrap up on creating your Rules for Mom!

Now that I clarified why we need Rules for ourselves, we're going to keep today short and sweet.

Part of your assignment for today is going to be to develop Rules for your pain points and then adopt those Rules. But I have some additional suggestions for you about *how* you're going to adopt these Rules for yourself.

First of all, you could come up with a dozen or more Rules for yourself, but if a dozen Rules sounds overwhelming to you, or if you've come up with Rules that you suspect you won't be able to commit to, then developing the Rules in the first place is a wasted exercise. So, I'm going to ask you to simply develop and adopt a few Rules – *for now* – that you know you can stick to.

And, if adopting even a few Rules at once still seems overwhelming to you, pick the ONE Rule for yourself that you think will make the biggest impact on your parenting. Just adopt just that ONE. Again, adopt the ONE "for now." As you gain momentum and confidence, you can add in additional Rules to support you, one or two at a time.

Finally, the second part of your assignment has to do with *how* you will adopt your new Rules for yourself and commit to them. Most moms are reluctant to do this at first, but I can tell you that they later report back to me how happy they are that they did! Here it is:

Get up every morning, stand in front a mirror, and declare your Rules for yourself to yourself.

Yes, really! Let me tell you a few things about declaring your Rules aloud and talking to yourself in the mirror. When I started my system, I did this every morning. I stood in front of the mirror and spoke all ten of my commandments out loud. And I said them with *conviction*. You think it's hard to get your kids to take you seriously? Well, let me tell you - they are not going to take you seriously if you don't even take yourself seriously! You deserve for everyone in your home to take you seriously. You have to be able to say them like you mean it. The title of "Mother" is – or should be – an *honored* position!

Also, like anything that is new and unfamiliar, anything that changes an existing pattern, is going to feel really weird at first. But I want to emphasize "at first."

Here's a little experiment to demonstrate my point. Put this book down and cross your arms across your chest. Before you pick the book back up, notice which arm is on top and which is underneath. I'll wait….

Got it? Now put the book back down again and cross your arms again, but this time, put the *opposite* arm on top. I'll wait again….

Doesn't that feel weird? But why? They're *your* arms. They've been attached to your body your whole life. But suddenly, you probably had difficulty doing what I asked of you. And did you have to really think about it before you could cross them with the opposite arm on top? Did you even realize, before just now, that you always put the same arm on top and the same underneath when you cross your arms?! But you also know, that if you decided that you wanted to cross your arms the other way, you could practice until it came naturally, and it would no longer feel weird.

Declaring your Rules for Mom aloud in front of the mirror is a bit like that, as is developing the habit of sticking to your Rules. It takes practice. But you won't have to declare your Rules to yourself for long. Do you think I still say my Rules aloud in front of a mirror every morning? Of course not! I don't need to anymore. I've been committed to them for so long that they're part of my Mom DNA now. You only need to say them to yourself until it feels like the most natural thing in the world to you. Once the thought of a NO turning into a YES feels WEIRD to you, you are done. Once you're like, "why in the world would a no ever turn into a yes?", then you have graduated. Make sense? Plus, once the whole system, incorporating all Five Pillars, is put into place, everyone catches on quickly (including you!) that things are very different – and much better – in your home.

Repeating your Rules to yourself every day in the mirror is a *Signature Move* of my System because it helps you to take yourself seriously. And reinforcing them with yourself daily also helps *you* to keep them top of mind, so that you don't fall back into your old patterns. And if you DO fall back into an old pattern, don't panic! Just course correct yourself after you break one of your Rules. For example, if – like Jessica did for a while – you ask a question instead of giving a direction, either before or after your child responds with 'no,' simply repeat it as an instruction, such as, "What I meant to say was, 'Pick up your toys now.'"

As always, remember that "Practice makes progress"!

Day 18 Assignment:

- Routines!
    - o Your kids should be "getting it" by now. Continue to provide just enough support to keep them on track! Pull back to only the bare minimum. If they no longer need ANY support, just smile and Sprinkle!
- Rhythms!
    - o Same as above!
- Rules!
    - o For each pain point you came up with for your assignment on Day 17, write down a Rule for *you* that would help alleviate the pain point.
    - o Commit to *at least* ONE of your Rules for Mom that you can unwaveringly stick to. If you only pick ONE (or two or three) from your list, simply promise yourself that you will add in the other Rules you came up with as you gain confidence!
    - o Starting today, *declare* your Rules for Mom to yourself in front of a mirror.

o This one probably doesn't require a reminder (as I suspect you'll want to do this when no one is in earshot!), but do not tell your kids that these are your new Rules for Mom, just institute them or introduce them with, "From now on…"

Day 19:
Pillar 3 Rules – Creating Your House Rules: Start with Values

Today's Overview
- *Signature Moves*
  - o Rules based on values
  - o Criteria for sound Rules
- What you'll need
  - o Your journal for the assignment

"When your values are clear to you, making decisions becomes easier."

~Roy E. Disney

Have you ever seen the wall hangings and other décor items that say:

"In this house, we do second chances. We do grace. We do real. We do mistakes. We do 'I'm sorry.' We do loud. We do hugs. We do family. We do love."

I read that and thought they were utopian-like Rules, like, "YES! This is exactly how I feel about my home and how I want us to feel as a family." I thought whoever created that list poked around my heart and brain to come up with it. I really WANTED those to be the Rules of my house. I wanted my home to have that kind of *vibe*. So, I hung those Rules on the wall and made them the Rules of my house.

But guess what. Those could *not be* Rules in my home. It was chaos! I'd given them permission to basically do whatever they wanted without creating any boundaries around it! Although it's a great list, trying to make them our Rules turned the house into free-for-all! I needed to start over.

(The good news is that even though they are not our *Rules*, by establishing some real, clear Rules (and the rest of my System), that list is more like a description of how we live and how we feel in our house now. (But they are still not our *Rules*.) .)

Let's talk about what effective Rules for you home look like. Yet another *Signature Move* within The Stress-free Family System is that Rules meet the following criteria:

- Specific
- Measurable
- Actionable
- Consistent
- Tied to your family's values

It's much easier for children to behave the way we want them to when they are crystal clear on what the Rules are and what our expectations are of them. And that's the trouble. Many homes have Rules, but sometimes they're loosely defined and loosely followed. Sometimes a behavior is okay, and other times it's not. The Rules could be totally dependent on whether mom can "deal with it" today or if she simply "cannot even." This goes back to consistency.

What we are going to do together, is come up with some Rules for your home that you will *commit* to enforcing. Rules that feel important enough that you will follow through on them ALL of the time. Which is why I love my *Signature Move* of tying Rules to your principles and values. It's much easier to be consistent with Rules for your children and your home when the Rules are grounded in teaching your kids concepts like respect, honor, and responsibility. It makes more sense to you, and it makes more sense to them, as well. They'll begin to understand that the Rules are there to guide and protect everyone, that they are helpful, and that they are *not* some arbitrary set of 'do's' and 'don'ts' that Mom came up with, just to let them know who's boss. So, we are going to work on creating Rules based on the values that we want to live by and the values we want to instill in our children!

The Rules become the external boundaries that we expect them to live within, but it's the values and the principals that we really want to reinforce in them. The good stuff. Ultimately, we want them to be internally motivated to do what's right and to develop strong principles and values.   This all starts at home.

So what kind of people are you hoping to raise? What values do you want to promote in your home? Kindness? Dependability? Honesty? Respect?

Spend a little quiet time coming up with a list of the core values you want to instill in your children and you want them to live by, both in and beyond your home. That is, list the values that are *most* important to you and your family. If you need some inspiration, do a quick internet search for "core values list" or "list of personal values." You'll find a ton of ideas there.

Once you get clarity on the most important values to live by for your family, we'll work on tying them to your Rules for your home.

Day 19 Assignment:
- Routines – Keep at them!
- Rhythms – Are you feeling the ease?

- Rules!
  - o Did you stick to the Mom Rule(s) you committed to? Did you declare them in the mirror today? Don't skip this step!
  - o Make a list of your top, or core, values and write them in your journal. Tomorrow we'll work on the Rules that go with them!

Day 20:
Pillar 3 Rules – Values-Based Rules for Kids and Home

Today's Overview:
- Signature Moves
  - o Rules based on values
  - o Sprinkling
- What you'll need
  - o Your journal for today's assignment

"My parents taught me about the importance of qualities like kindness, respect, and honesty, and I realize how central values like these have been to me throughout my life."

~Kate Middleton, Mother of three, Duchess of Cambridge, and likely future queen consort

Yes! The values and principles you instill in your children will stay with them for life. And you could talk about values all the live-long day, but in order for your children to learn to *live* those values, they need to *do* something. They need to *practice*. And don't you want to eventually send them out into the world with a solid foundation based on practice, from home where it's safe? Of course, you do! I believe it's every parent's highest hopes for their children – that we will send them out into the world equipped to take care of themselves and to be good people.

Your children will practice your values by adhering to the Rules you establish, based on those values. Their everyday activities and Routines will be steeped in solid values that they will carry with them to school, to playdates, to extracurricular activities, and into the world beyond. You will learn to weave your values and principals into everyday conversation with your kids, using their behavior as teaching moments. Doesn't that sound great?

So how do we create Rules based on values? It's very simple.

With your list of core values handy, you're going to think through any existing Rules you have in your house and see how they apply to those values. Then, you'll review your values again and develop any additional Rules you may need in your house to reinforce those values.

For example, my client Christine had a Rule in her house that her children needed to share their toys with each other, as well as with any friends or other guests they might have. When she looked at the values she'd listed, she thought that rule applied to two of her core values: "community" and "kindness." You'll find that most Rules will reinforce more than one value, which is great! Sometimes she can reinforce the value of kindness by saying things like, "In our family, we are kind to each other, so we share our toys politely with others." Another time, she can enforce the Rule while emphasizing the value of community by saying, "Our family is a community, and people in a good community share their toys."

Let's say that Christine's values list also includes "respect." Respect comes from treating *yourself*, other people, and property well. She could apply this value to any Rules she has about cleaning up. For example, she might say, "In our home, we respect our property. Please put your toys away." To reinforce a different Rule with the same value, she could tell her kids, "Our family respects our house and the things and people in it. Please sweep up the mess you tracked in when you kept your shoes on when you came home from school." Christine feels like a *great* mom, instead of a mean mom, when she enforces the Rules now, because she knows she not only keeping order in her home, but also teaching her kids important values and life skills at the same time! It sure makes it easier to be consistent and enforce rules at home when it makes us feel like we're doing a great job as a mom.

Yes, the *primary* reason you want your kids to put their toys away or to sweep the floor might be that you don't want to have a messy house. But the bigger picture is that they learn to put things away for themselves and to be respectful of their things. Can you think of other important values that could be tied to a simple Rule like 'pick up your toys'? How about *independence, cleanliness,* or *gratitude.* You get the idea!

So, when you think about the Rules that you want to have for your home and for your children, you are making Rules about *behaviors,* but your *speaking to* the *values* that you tie the Rules back to.

Let me help you get started by putting some of those values into buckets with their corresponding Rules.

- We want our kids to be kind and nice, right? Taking turns, sharing, being supportive are all behaviors that could come under *kindness* or *niceness.*
- We want your children to listen while others speak –without interrupting or talking back. These things fall under *respect.*
- We want them to go to bed on time, eat healthy, and stand up for themselves. These would be examples of *self-respect, confidence,* or *health.*
- We want them to share in household responsibilities and help, support, and stand up for each other. That's *teamwork,* which could also be *community*!

Do you see? When you think about the Rules or expectations you want for your children and your home, think in terms of principles, core values, and character. Use those words and then drill down to the behaviors. That way, when the behaviors show up, you can speak to the values they represent and that way, the Rule and the value reinforce one another like magic!

You see, once you identify what core values YOU want to drive home, you use them as a bucket or as an umbrella to keep the conversation going when you need to speak about a Rule. You just need to decide what the handful of values are that you will weave into those conversations.

And of course, I'm always going to suggest *sprinkling* commentary that promotes your agenda! For example, if you value "tidiness," after your kids put their toys away, you might say, "Tidiness is so important. Doesn't it look so much nicer in your room now? It's so relaxing when your toys are put away and everything is so orderly. Plus, we'll know where your toys are when you're ready to play with them next time. Thank you."

Are you getting the hang of it now? It's time to start building out your Rules for your kids and your Rules for your home. Similar to what I asked you to do with your Rules of Mom, I'd like to ask you to begin with the values and Rules you feel most strongly about. Commit to some Kid Rules and values and some House Rules and values that matter most to you first. These will be easier to commit to following through on, *even when* you're tired, busy, or distracted. Then you will get the confidence that comes with practice to add more values-based Rules for your kids and your home, as you go. But unlike Rules for Mom which you implemented immediately, you will not be implementing Kids Rules or House Rules yet. You'll have to wait until the last Pillar, Revolutionize, when you have your family meeting and your kids will have the opportunity to create the Rules for themselves and their home!

Day 20 Assignment:

- Routines – Do you even need to reinforce them now? Are your kids getting them all by themselves? A smile, a nod, a high five may be all you need by now!

- Rhythms – Do you agree with most of my clients that this is the *best* thing about The System?

- Rules!

  o Declare your Rules for Mom in the mirror – and keep sticking to them. Is it time to add another?

  o Consider the Rules and values most important to you. Write down your "dream" Rules for your kids and your home and how you can link them to the three values or principles that are also the most important to you.

  o Think about things you can say and things you can do to reinforce those values when each Rule comes up in your house.

- Get ready for Pillar 4: Rewards!

Day 21:
Pillar 4 Rewards – Introduction to
REWARDS

Today's Overview

- *Signature Moves*
    - o The Three C's
    - o Relevant Consequences
    - o "Sprinkle" around what your family has accomplished so far
    - *o Shhh!* It's still a secret.
- What you'll need
    - o Your journal for the assignment

"You get what you reward. Be clear about what you want to get and systematically reward it."

~Dr. Bob Nelson, best-selling author and motivational speaker

Welcome to Pillar 4, Rewards! A quick check-in before we jump in.

How has it been going so far? The Routines and Rhythms should be close to being on autopilot by now, which means you should already be seeing big changes at home: Easier mornings, calmer evenings, yes?

Now, what about how *you* are doing? Have you been speaking your Rules to yourself in the mornings? Have you been speaking your Rules to yourself in the moment? Are they starting to become second nature? If you've been consistent with the Rules you've adopted for yourself, are you ready to add a new one? If you are, then go for it. Pick a Rule for yourself that you can be consistent with and that will make a significant difference in your home. If you're not ready yet, no problem! Just check in periodically and see if you are ready to add another Rule for yourself that will help move you closer to your goal.

And of course, keep practicing ALL of it. Every bit of it needs to feel natural – every Routine, every Rhythm, every Rule.

Okay, let's get to Rewards! I love, love, LOVE creating Reward Systems because – done right –the Reward System is what keeps your home on track. Rewards encourage your kids to follow all of the Routines, Rhythms, and Rules you've been so busy creating and to follow everything consistently and independently. I hope you are as excited as I am to dive into Rewards!

For the most part, the Stress-Free Family works on a Reward System to regulate behavior. However, we do use two types of consequences, when necessary. But before we dole out a consequence, we need to make sure that it's appropriate and justified. To determine appropriate consequences, we need to start with the expectation. The expectation is the behavior we want, right? The consequence occurs when the expectation is not met. But before we give our children consequences, we need to make sure that there are a few things in place.

1. We need to make sure that the expectation is realistic. That is, ensure your child is literally capable of doing what it is you're requiring of them. Whether the expectation is to sit quietly in the car for 30 minutes or to pack up their Tomorrow Box without any prompts, the expectation needs to be attainable. Does your child struggle with executive function?

The executive functions are the parts of thinking and reasoning that help us manage ourselves and get things done. If executive function is a challenge for your child, then expecting them to keep an orderly backpack and check it monthly is not realistic. Expecting them to follow a checklist of what needs to be in the backpack and check it daily is realistic. Yes?

2. Once you are sure that your expectation can realistically be met, make sure your child understands exactly what it is you expect of them by delivering the instruction using the *Signature Move* of The Three C's of communication. In a **calm** manner, give them **clear, concise** instructions. Begin by using their name – to get their attention –then use as few words as necessary to explain what needs to be done. Don't leave any room for miscommunication about the expectation – *what* you want them to do and *when*. For example, "Mary put away your toys now." Get it? Too many moms use too many words to communicate what they expect to happen. With smaller children or kids who get distracted easily, this is even more critical. Some kids need to be given instructions using as little as two or three words. Keep it as simple as possible. "Mary Brush teeth now," or "Johnny toys away now." Keep it super simple.

3. Next, if you know the expectation is realistic AND you've been *calm, clear,* and *concise* with your delivery, yet they are not meeting the expectation, unfortunately, a consequence may be necessary.

I really prefer to focus on setting your children up to behave well and be able to Reward them, but sometimes a consequence is necessary, let's address it now. We want to make sure that if we have to give consequences that we're doing it in the most effective way possible.

I know that in some homes, consequences take the form of taking away privileges, such as canceling a weekend play date or taking away screen time. Or consequences show up as yelling, screaming, threatening, or punishing their kids into behaving well. *I don't want you to go down that road.* Do you know why? Because moms who nag, yell, scream, threaten, or punish their kids into behaving are just plain miserable. No mom wants to be yelling at their kids all the time. And no mom wants their kids spending their life in time out, right? And because your kids aren't learning to follow directions when they're given. They are learning to react to nagging, yelling, screaming, threatening and/or punishing. We definitely don't want that!

To be clear, I'm not saying that punishment is *never* warranted. There may be times when punishment is the best strategy. However, when punishment is used as the PRIMARY means to get your child to do what you want them to do, then they are operating from a place of fear. For example, "I'm not going to hit my brother because mom will take away screen time," or "I'm not going to tell mom I didn't hand in homework because I'm going to lose a playdate." See what can happen? They may start lying to mom to avoid being punished, in essence, controlling their behavior to avoid punishment. What we want is to have them learn to do the right things and avoid making bad choices. Punishment often leads to making decisions based on whether or not they'll get caught doing something or whether or not they'll be punished for it, instead of listening to their inner guidance.

What we are working toward is helping our children develop that inner guidance system! So yes, in the short term, punishment may work for you. But we want to play the long game! It's more important for them to practice making decisions based on internal motivation rather than external. We'd rather have our kids deciding not to do something because they know it's inappropriate rather than not doing it because they'll miss out on screen time, right?

The Stress-Free Family doesn't use punishments as a form of behavior management. We use two types of *signature* consequences. The first type is a R*elevant* Consequence. A Relevant Consequence is a consequence that is a natural outcome of an infraction of a known expectation. For example, if the Tomorrow Box is not properly packed in the evening, your child may forget to pack his cleats for soccer. A naturally occurring consequence is being unable to play soccer. If your child leaves their wet towel on the floor and doesn't pick it up after a gentle reminder, a Relevant Consequence would be to have him or her to do a load of laundry, as you now need clean towels. Get the idea? Typically, when Relevant Consequences are given, you get a bit of a two-for-one. There's usually an additional, naturally occurring consequence because having to perform the consequence (e.g., doing the laundry) means they'll also miss out on something they'd rather do. Time spent in the laundry room means they are not playing outside, enjoying their screen time, or doing something else they enjoy. They are wasting *their* time by needing to correct their behavior.

Here's an example of a Relevant Consequence my client Elaine used one day when her daughter Sophie was being disrespectful. She first explained to Sophie that being disrespectful to her parents and others was unacceptable. Then she told Sophie that she'd be calling her friend Olivia's mom to let them know that Sophie would not be able to sleep over at Olivia's house this weekend, as planned. But before she made the call, she clarified to Sophie that the reason she was no longer permitted to go to the sleepover was that she needed Sophie to be able to demonstrate respectful behavior at home before she'd be allowed to visit someone else's home. That is, Elaine needed to be confident that Sophie would be respectful to her friends and their parents before she sent her to visit another family.

Yes, Elaine took a privilege away, but there was a *context* for that. Elaine connected the dots for Sophie. She made a link between the need to be respectful (is that one of your family values?!)

and the privilege of spending time with friends. She was tuning Sophie into that inner guidance system.

The Relevant Consequence makes it easier for them to be clear on *why* they got the consequence. There's a logical connection between their behavior and the consequence that they can understand. It needs to make sense to them in order for the consequence to be effective in encouraging the good behavior. It's easier for your children to learn because they already understand the concept of cause and effect. If Elaine were to have punished Sophie by taking away screen time, that wouldn't have made sense to Sophie, because the punishment would have seemed random. When the consequence is relevant, it seems almost obvious!

So, as much as I'd love to be getting you started right away on your Rewards system, it's important to have you get started with thinking about the typical infractions that occur in your home and begin to think about what the logical, relevant consequences would be for your child. You need to be ready when those infractions occur so that you don't end up with punishments or consequences that are unrelated to the infraction.

Although consequences are sometimes necessary, most research says that positive motivation achieves better results than punishing. Therefore, whenever possible, use motivating words to encourage good behavior. Of course, I have a few strategies up my sleeve that I am going to share with you in the upcoming days!

Day 21 Assignment:

- Routines – I hope your kids have them down pat by now! If not, keep reinforcing - but use as little prompting as possible. And don't forget to "Sprinkle" in the benefits!

- Rhythms – Same as above! I hope they're going well!

- Rules!

- o Keep declaring your Rules for Mom in the mirror. You want to really make them a part of your Mom DNA. Stick to them and add Rules as appropriate.
- Rewards!
  - o I know, I know. We're in Pillar 4 Rewards, but we didn't get to talk about them yet. Rewards are coming, and I promise it's going to be amazing. But for now, your assignment is to grab your journal, make a list of common infractions in your home (i.e., where your expectations aren't being met), and come up with a Relevant Consequence for each.

Day 22:
Pillar 4 Rewards - Reinforce Good Behavior with TRIBE

Today's Overview

- *Signature Moves*
  - o The "TRIBE" method of reinforcement
    - ▪ Precision of praise
  - o Relevant Consequences
- What you'll need
  - o Your journal for your assignment

"Recognition is not a scarce resource.
You can't use it up or run out of it."

~Susan M. Heathfield, About.com Human Resources Expert

Let's recap!

On Day 21, we covered one of the two types of consequences we use within The Stress-Free Family System. We'll get to the second one, which is directly connected to the Rewards System you'll be building, shortly. But we left off with the need for motivating words that encourage good behavior from our children. And I promised you some tips!

The first is a very effective strategy and a *Signature Move* that I call "TRIBE." TRIBE stands for Time, Recognition, Importance, Benefit, and Encouragement. Let me break down how to use the TRIBE method.

1. Find ways to praise directly in real *Time* by catching them in the act of meeting your expectation.

2. Acknowledge your child by showing them that you *Recognize* the good behavior.

3. Explain the *Importance* of the good behavior as part of the bigger picture.

4. Point out the *Benefit* of the desired behavior.

5. End with some words of *Encouragement*.

Let's walk through this with an example. Let's pretend that you have an expectation that, in your home, everyone takes their shoes off when they walk in the door, and everyone has a spot for their shoes in the mudroom. This is what an opportunity to praise in real time sounds like.

"Billy, I noticed you lined your shoes up in the mudroom as soon as you walked in the door, that will help keep our floors clean. Now you can enjoy your TV time without being interrupted because you won't have to help me sweep! I appreciate you remembering to do that, thank you."

Simple, right? The moment you see them doing something well, start with their name to signal that you are speaking to them, then recognize the behavior by saying you noticed they lined their shoes up in the mudroom as soon as they came inside.

- **TIME** – Start as soon as the shoes are put away.

- **RECOGNITION** – Restate the behavior you want them to repeat – putting the shoes away.

- **IMPORTANCE** – Explain how their behavior relates to the bigger picture – it helps keep the floor clean.

- **BENEFIT** – State what's in it for them – they aren't wasting their time sweeping up (which would be the *Relevant Consequence* if the shoes weren't put away).

- **ENCOURAGEMENT** – Give them positive attention that re-inforces the good behavior – "Thank you." Or, "I really appre-ciate it."

Don't overlook the power of using the TRIBE strategy instead of only saying 'thank you' or 'great job.' Generic phrases like that are not going to get your kids to repeat the good behavior. It may seem obvi-ous to you what you're acknowledging or thanking them for, but if you want to see the precise behavior repeated, you need to spell it out for them.

You have to connect all the dots. Tie the praise to the specific be-havior, then tie the specific behavior to the bigger picture, and connect it to the benefit to them. Remember how important linking is. Your children need to know specifically what they did to get that positive reaction from you. When you detail what they did well, they'll know what to repeat and when. Adding the explanation of why it's import-ant within the bigger picture, lets them know WHY they should re-peat the behavior. Reminding them that they'll get to avoid dealing with the Relevant Consequences helps them connect the benefits to their good behavior. And ending it all with an encouraging phrase will leave them feeling good. The TRIBE method perfectly positions your child *for success* – to behave well in return for positive attention from you.

When your child is doing what they are supposed to be doing, you'll have the right words ready to encourage them to keep it up. Another strategy to motivate your kids to repeat good behavior is positive attention in the form of extended eye contact, a big smile, a high five or a nod of the head. These are easy to do and believe it or not, can go a long way to motivate kids. Kids are always naturally looking for attention, they're going to go for what gets them the big-gest bang. The question is: Will it be negative attention or positive attention?

Try to heap on the positive attention as much as possible and try to dial down the negative. The Stress-Free Family System's philosophy eliminates nagging, yelling, screaming, and punishing. The last thing you want is to engage in a power struggle with your kids, right? I'm guessing you've 'been there done that' and know how frustrating and ineffective it is.

Your kids have the power to decide. Will they decide to misbehave, be disrespectful, and not meet your expectations? Or will they decide to behave, be respectful, and cooperate? You know what encourages the latter decision? Keeping your cool and giving them Relevant Consequences for misbehavior and motivating them towards good behavior. The Stress-Free Family System does a great job of creating the structure for good behavior. It sets you and your children up *for success*.

REMEMBER: Continue to keep the details behind The Stress-Free Family System a secret!

Once the Rewards System is in effect, your home will really be humming along. But we just needed to address why we use Rewards instead of punishments and praise instead of yelling. So, now that I got that out of the way – *Whew!* – let's create a Rewards System where you won't even have to think about punishing your kids ever again. Ready?

Day 22 Assignment:
- Routines! Your Routines should require little to no maintenance by now. Do only what you need to do in order to keep them going.
- Rhythms! Now that things are moving more smoothly in your home, has it helped you to notice anywhere that you still have a 'hiccup'? Don't be afraid to introduce new Rhythms!
- Rules!

o Declare your Rules for Mom in the mirror!

o Add Rules as needed.

- Rewards!

  o For common infractions, write out in your journal a TRIBE script for the next time you "catch" your kids meeting your expectations! (Then don't be surprised when you find that you need to use Relevant Consequences less and less!)

  o Practice administering Relevant Consequences for the common infractions, as they arise.

Day 23:
Pillar 4 Rewards – Expectations and Intervals for Rewards System

Today's Overview:

- Signature Moves
  - o Consequences tied to Rewards System
  - o Weekly "payday"
  - o Keeping it a secret from the kids
  - o A system that is Complete and Integrated
- What you'll need
  - o Your journal

"Instead of yelling and spanking, which don't work anyway, I believe in finding creative ways to keep their attention - turning things into a game, for instance. And, when they do something good, positive reinforcement and praise."

~Patricia Richardson, American actress best known for her portrayal of Jill Taylor on "Home Improvement"

Let's keep going with the Rewards Pillar – we're finally getting to the good part! On Day 21, I explained that we use only two types of consequences in The Stress-Free Family System, and we covered the first type, which was Relevant Consequences. Relevant Consequences cover all the in-the-moment consequences for misbehavior, infractions, or not meeting expectations.

The second type of consequence is a *lack* of privileges within the Reward System. That is, we are going to create a Reward System where the kids *earn* privileges for meeting expectations. Their consequence for failing to meet expectations is the lack of privileges, which we are going to build into the Rewards System. We won't be taking anything *away*, they just aren't earning it if they don't meet the expectations. In this way, we are empowering them to behave better.

But I want to make something very clear. I am not talking about bribing. I know a lot of moms use bribes as Rewards, and believe me, I was guilty of that too! My *Signature* Rewards System is not about bribes. It's built to set up a real structure of known Rewards for known behaviors. Rewards that are expected because they've been earned, not an in-the-moment bribe. Getting kids to behave becomes much easier when we create an atmosphere of privileges that correlate to excellent behavior – we make the privileges *relevant* to The System, just as we make the consequences relevant to the infractions. And that's what we're going to do for your home starting right now. Another *Signature Move* of The Stress-free Family System is that we integrate all the parts of The System. So, when we build your Reward System, their Rewards will be based upon the successful completion of their Routines, their participation in the Rhythms and their adherence to the Rules!

Before we dive into the Rewards Systems set up, you will need to consider how this will work for *your* family. For example, how you set up your system will depend, in part, on how many children you have, as well as their ages. My three kids are pretty close in age, and they all enjoy the same activities and want to be rewarded in the same way, so I've been able to use the exact same Rewards System with all of them. That is, the expectations I've set are realistic, attainable, and appropriate for all three of them. And they are all working towards earning the same Rewards. Therefore, I only need one system.

If you have children who are differently abled, are motivated by very different things, or there is a large age difference among them, you may have to either design a Rewards System for each of them or create one Rewards System but modify the expectations for each child. This will become clearer as you keep reading. And I'll be going over a complete Rewards System later in the book, with examples, so that will help, as well.

So, now you know that you need to decide if you're creating one Rewards System that will work for all of your children or that you may have to tailor your Rewards System to suit your children's different needs. The next two things you need to know are that your new Rewards System will be based on a "currency" and that you will have to decide what interval you want your system to operate under.

The currency will be what they will be earning when they meet and exceed expectations. In what "form" will your currency be? In my home, I use beads. To keep it simple, I'll be referring to beads throughout my explanation of Rewards. But you can use something you have on hand or pick another form of currency - but sorting that out isn't critical right now. We'll talk more about it in a bit!

As for the interval, think of it like a weekly paycheck for your child, where each week starts a new cycle of earning. You must decide if you'd prefer for the currency to be earned during a five-day (i.e., school day) schedule or a seven-day schedule. This is an important distinction, so you need to think about how your kids' lives are scheduled, what they are capable of, and how you'd like your home to run. Moms whose homes have a set weekday schedule – of school and activities – but their weekends are less structured, often set up a five-day schedule. This is how I run the Rewards System in my home. My kids earn during the school week, and then they have two days "off," just like most adults would experience with a workweek. A five-day interval begins on Sunday evening when they pack Tomorrow Boxes for Monday, and it ends when they come home and put the Tomorrow Box in its place on Friday afternoon.

However, some homes have scheduled activities on the weekends, just as they do during the week. As a result, the kids in those homes need to stick to preparing their Tomorrow Boxes at night and stick to their Routines over the weekend just as they do during the school week. Moms in homes like this set up a seven-day Rewards system. Also, moms who have kids who do better with more structure often adopt a seven-day schedule, even if their weekends aren't very scheduled. It can help keep kids on track by making every day of the week consistent in terms of Routines and expectations.

For example, my client Leslie wanted to operate on a five-day, school week interval for her family. She has four children, aged five to twelve, and they are involved in activities that take place on the weekend, too. Leslie noticed that she began dreading Saturdays and Sundays! They felt like the mornings they *used* to have every day before she implemented The 28-Day Stress-Free Family System – with nagging and chaos and being late for activities. And you know how that made her feel? *Like a bad mom!* The weekend is for family time. The weekend is supposed to be fun! Yet she hated it more than Monday! She realized that, because of the weekend activity schedule, her kids needed the structure that their Monday-Friday Routines provided for them. So, she adjusted to a seven-day interval. Her kids now know to follow their Routines, complete with Tomorrow Box preparation, every day of the week. As soon as she made the change, things calmed down for Leslie's family's weekends. (And she feels like a good mom again!)

If you aren't sure whether the five- or seven-day interval is right for your home and your kids, one good indicator that your child can take the weekend "off" is whether or not they easily Transition back into the school week on Mondays. Also, if they seem to find it more challenging to behave according to expectations on Saturdays and Sundays, the seven-day interval is likely the best bet for your home.

Most homes will have either a five- or seven-day Rewards interval, but if things are a little different in your home, based on work schedules, school schedules, and other activities, feel free to adopt what makes the most sense for a typical week in your home!

This weekly cycle will determine your children's Main Reward, which is the central part of the overall Rewards system. In the days ahead, we will get into more detail about how your Routines and expectations allow your children to earn their Main Reward each week – OR how falling short of expectations leads to the consequence of failing to earn their Main Reward.

Also coming up, we will clarify how there are actually five levels of Rewards, which will be based upon your children's ages and abilities, as well as your preferences, and how the other levels tie into the overall system.

In the next few days, we will

- Review all five levels of Rewards.
- Determine whether you need to use all five, or if two or three will be effective for your home. (The weekly and Main Reward apply to all Rewards systems.)
- Identify what is Rewarding (and therefore motivating) to your children.
- Clarify how expectations are tied to Rewards.
- Connect the dots between how meeting expectations leads to Rewards earned and how falling short of expectations leads to the consequence of not receiving the Rewards.

Day 23 Assignment:
- Routines & Rhythms – Stick with them!
- Rules!

- o Declare your Rules for Mom in the mirror!
- o Add Rules as needed.
- Rewards!
  - o Think through your weekly schedule and determine whether a five- or seven-day Rewards payout system will work best for your family.

Day 24:
Pillar 4 Rewards – Types and Timing of Rewards

Today's Overview

- *Signature Moves*
  - o Consequences tied to Rewards system
  - o Five Levels of Rewards
- What you'll need
  - o Your journal
  - o Unit of "currency" [Explained today; needed by Day 28]
  - o Containers for currency supply and each child's "earnings" [Also not needed until Day 28]

"The cost of praising someone is nil - but every psychological study shows the payoff is huge."

~Harvey Mackay, businessman, author and syndicated columnist

Yesterday (Day 23), you decided on a weekly interval for the Main Rewards in your home. I mentioned that it was like your kids will receive a weekly paycheck for sticking to their Routines and Rhythms and following the Rules to earn their Main Reward. But my *Signature Move* is to use up to five levels of Rewards, so your kids may have additional payouts, as well. Let's review these Reward levels now!

Permission Slip to Skip! If you have smaller children, you may find that you need to use all five Rewards levels in your family's system. But if your children are older, you may need to introduce only two or three of them. I recommend that you read through all five levels to determine what makes the most sense for your family. But then you have my permission to only apply the Rewards levels that make sense for your family and to skip the others.

Levels of Rewards

1. <u>Micro Rewards</u> – Very small Rewards, given multiple times a day; Apply to very young children.

2. <u>Mini Rewards</u> – Small, daily Rewards given at the end of the day; Apply to younger children.

3. <u>Main Rewards</u> – Rewards that are earned every five- or seven-day week for meeting the basic expectations of the family's system; EVERY Rewards Systems must have this.

4. <u>Major Rewards</u> – Rewards that are earned every five- or seven-day week for ***exceeding*** the basic expectations of the family's system; Should be incorporated in ***all*** Rewards Systems.

5. <u>Mega Rewards</u> – "High-ticket" Rewards items that require "banking" of some weekly Rewards to save up for the Reward; Mega Rewards are more easily implemented for older, more mature children, but can be used for younger children, as well.

Let's go back to the weekly paycheck analogy to clarify the "***when***" for each level of Rewards before we get into the ***"what"*** that Reward level might look like.

Think of all the ways that adults can be paid for their work:

- Weekly
- Every two weeks
- Twice a month

- Once a month (this is typical in Europe!)
- Daily (e.g., a dog walker)
- Per project (e.g., when a graphic artist completes a job)
- Annually (e.g., company bonus)

There are probably more examples, but you get the idea. For your kids, their "work" is their good behavior and meeting your expectations. Their "pay" comes in the form of their Rewards. Can you see how the pay intervals in the list above won't all work for children? Adults who receive an annual bonus at the end of the year might be motivated to work hard all year to maximize that bonus check. But imagine telling an eight-year-old that they'll get a Reward if they're good *all year*. It doesn't matter how big that Reward might be, eight-year-olds aren't capable of waiting all year to earn Rewards. Which is why we need the Main Reward schedule as well as a few other tricks, depending on our kids.

A single payday every week will probably work well for capable children of about 8-years and older. That is, if you tell your 8-year-old that they will earn a treat after behaving well for a week, they can probably delay gratification until the end of the week to receive that Reward. For younger children, the weekly payout works well, but they may also need some additional incentives to encourage them through the whole week, which is where daily Mini and Micro Rewards come in.

Let's talk about how **Micro** and **Mini Rewards** work. If you have a very young child or one who's very easily distracted, you may need to use a Micro Reward after each Routine/Transition throughout the day. So, your child would receive a Micro Reward after a successful Morning Routine, another after a successful Afternoon Routine, and a third after a successful Evening Routine. Some moms even find that they need to add a Micro Reward for each *Cluster* of activities within a Transition – for example, the bathroom portion of the Morning Routine – for very young children. Soon, we'll work on figuring out the types of things that motivate your children. But to give an example for now, if your child does best being Rewarded after each Transition, that might look like earning 10 minutes of playing games on their tablet.

Mini Rewards are Rewards that are paid out at the end of a successful day. Mini Rewards can be used as an additional incentive for children who are given Micro Rewards to help encourage them to get through the whole day. They can also be used for kids who do not need Micro Rewards at each Transition, but for whom waiting all week to be Rewarded may be a challenge.

For all children, we want to Reward them for meeting weekly expectations with the **Main Reward**. But we also want to encourage them to go above and beyond and to help them fine tune that internal guidance system. That's where the **Major Reward** comes in – a little "bump" to the weekly Main Reward to sweeten the pot. Exceeding expectations will look different for different kids, but the concept is the same. Think of this as creating additional earning opportunities for exceptional behavior. For example, you can "catch" them doing something helpful or kind, beyond what's expected, and allow them to earn more currency toward their weekly Rewards. You can offer them more currency for higher school grades at school or for feeding a pet!

Finally, older children may be motivated by "high-ticket" items that may take several weeks or even months to earn. **Mega Rewards** don't have a specified interval but are paid out as enough currency is "banked" (we will get to banking on Day 25) to earn the Reward. As the name suggests, Mega Rewards are things that are "big," which means anything that's a big deal to both them and to you. For example, if your kids are motivated by tickets to sporting events, those take big money. If they'd like to host a group of friends for a sleepover, that's a big commitment.

Let's talk a little bit about the currency you'll use for your Rewards system. But first, please note that the currency does NOT apply to Micro Rewards as those are being given immediately when they are successful. They are used for Mini Rewards (if you choose to pay out daily) and for weekly success.

The currency you choose is up to you. You can even use checkmarks or a tally system if you want, but I highly recommend that you use something tangible for younger children. Angie, one of my clients, uses playing cards. It was something she had handy already, and it works just fine! Even though my kids are older, I set the system up when they were younger, so I still use the beads I started with! I liked the beads because I could use different colors for each kid (remember my color coding *Signature Move*?) and they make a satisfying little 'clink' when I drop them in their containers, as they earn Rewards. And that's a good segue to containers.

You will need a container for each child for their currency, as well as a container for where you keep the currency until it's been earned. Each time your child successfully completes a Routine, you'll take one unit of currency from your container and add it to theirs, in essence, "paying" them.

The currency simply needs to be something that can be counted, something easy to manage in its containers, and something that appeals in your household.

I just want to repeat that the currency will be earned daily, with the successful completion of each Routine. Therefore, if your family has three Transitions/Routines a day, and your child completes them all successfully, they would earn three units of currency for the day. At the end of a successful five-day week, they would have earned 15 units of currency for completing Routines. (In The System, there are ways to earn more than the minimum of 15, but we'll get to that on Day 25!).

Rhythms are folded into their Routines Transition time. So, for example, if you choose to use The Prime Time Rhythm, and it isn't adhered to, it's likely that in addition to the answer being "no" to whatever they ask, you will also be late for school, so the currency would not be earned.

To summarize, the currency is earned daily, but the Rewards are received weekly. Again, think about it as earning pay daily and getting a weekly paycheck.

On Day 25, we will get into motivators for your children and applying Major and Mega Rewards.

Day 24 Assignment:

- Routines & Rhythms – Keep them going, Mama!
- Rules!
  - o I encourage you to add another Rule from the list you came up with.
  - o Add the Rule and keep declaring your Rules in the mirror and in the moment!
- Rewards!
  - o Consider the ages and abilities of your children. Determine whether one or more of your children will require Micro and Mini Rewards in addition to the weekly Main Reward.
  - o Decide what your family will use for its currency, what containers you will use, and where they will be stored. Don't forget the container you'll use to hold the currency until it's been earned by the kids!

Day 25:
Pillar 4 Rewards – Tying Rewards to Motivators

Today's Overview
- Signature Moves
  - Five Levels of Rewards
  - Connecting Rewards and Motivation
  - Bonus currency for going above and beyond
  - "Banking" currency to earn Mega Rewards
  - Limiting ways to lose currency
- What you'll need
  - Your journal for recording the assignment
  - Don't forget to grab your currency supplies before Day 28!

"Motivation is what gets you started. Habit is what keeps you going."

~Jim Ryun, Olympic track silver medalist

I picked the quote above because I thought it really hit the nail on the head for where we are in this process right now. In this Pillar, we're talking about what motivates your kids and incorporating those motivators into your home's Reward System. At the same time, it should be getting clear by now – because you're already perfecting those Routines and Rhythms – that encouraging effective *habits* is what keeps your home on track. Adding the Rewards System is only going to further reinforce those good habits. It's still a secret for now, but once you implement the Rewards System in your home, you're going to be amazed at how effectively it works and how consistently your kids begin to meet your expectations and earn their Rewards! So, let's talk about what motivates *your* kids.

Micro and Mini Rewards

Some of you will be starting with **Micro** and **Mini Rewards**. The purpose of these is to give them *just* enough to tide them over until they get to the weekly, Main Reward. I like this food analogy: Think of the Main Reward as dinner time and Micro and Mini Rewards are like snacks. A snack needs to be "just right" – you don't want to give your child too much food and spoil their dinner. At the same time, you want to give them enough to prevent them from becoming irritable, cranky, and unable to focus – and from coming to ask you to fix them *another* snack before dinner! So, you offer them just enough to make it to dinner time.

If that's how Micro and Mini Rewards work, what should the Reward "snack" be? Earlier, I used the example of 10 minutes of tablet time. For some kids, getting that hit of tablet screen time before school might be all they need to motivate them to finish up their Morning Routine correctly and on time. So that could be one option. But not every child is motivated by tablets, or maybe you don't want your kids on the tablet before school. What will motivate your child?   I know my kids liked some time sorting their baseball cards, some kids like to listen to music or read a book, or little ones like to build with Legos. As they get older, they might want to check their phones for social media activity.

Whatever it is that they like to do, give it a time limit of 10 minutes and if they have completed their Morning Routine correctly and on time, that means they have 10 minutes for their Micro Reward. And, of course, since they have successfully completed their Morning Routines, they'll also earn one unit of currency for the Transition.

If your kids don't need Micro Rewards for each Transition but they do need a Mini Reward at the end of each day, then after successful Morning, Afternoon, and Evening Routines, they would get their Mini Reward – just before they go to bed, which would be the last step of a successful Evening Routine. Mini Rewards have more to do with timing than magnitude. So, they could be the same types of 10-minute Micro Rewards activities or they could be a little "bigger" since they've taken all day to earn. For example, a Mini Reward for the day might be 30 minutes of watching a favorite TV show, working on their card collection, listening to music, or playing a board game. Think of the Mini Reward as a small motivator at the end of a successful day that will encourage them to remember to move through their day successfully again *tomorrow*.

One thing I want to add before we move on to the Main Rewards. Your child will be earning one unit of currency for every Transition. So even if your child isn't getting any Micro or Mini Rewards, just the fact that they know they are earning something at every Transition IS a great motivator. Receiving recognition, from you, for every successful Transition, even if it's just a check on a dry erase board, will motivate your child to keep working towards their ultimate goal. I just wanted to clarify that all children are being motivated all throughout the day, even without the use of Micro and Mini Rewards.

Main Rewards

After you determine your Micro and Mini Rewards – if you will be using them – you need to figure out what your motivators will be as your child's Main Rewards.

The first thing we do when we start designing a Reward System is start with a clean slate. When you reveal the big picture to your family, as the last step in this process, everyone is given a fresh start, no matter what your home looked like "before." To do this, we start by taking the position that you are providing food, clothing, and housing for your child but everything else is a privilege. I know that sounds harsh but just stay with me. Your kids are going to get a lot of privileges, they'll just be earning them and will know what to expect instead of just expecting them with no rhyme or reason. When your kids are behaving well, and your home is running smoothly there will a ton of opportunities for fun!

Now, what are those things, those privileges, that will motivate your child to behave well all day, day after day, all week long? What is it that they like to do? Think about all of the privileges they enjoy, the things they do during their free time now. For example:

- Video game time
- Playdates after school
- Sleepovers
- Television time
- Going to the movies
- Tablet time
- Playing with their toys
- Playing games with you
- Pizza
- Special Dessert
- Bowling

Anything your kids enjoy doing counts as a privilege.

By the way, you can be very specific here. For example, if your child has a phone so that they can communicate with you and you know where they are, you may think of that as a necessity, rather than a privilege. I get that. But social media apps are not a necessity, right? Time to use social media or playing games on the phone could be a privilege.

Every single thing they like to do that is outside of what you need them to do is a privilege. To clarify, imagine that all your kids are doing is having breakfast, lunch, and dinner, showering, brushing their teeth, going to school, and any other "required" activities (e.g., religious or community service). If that was their whole life, what would they want to add back in?

These motivators you select need to be privileges that you are ready, willing and able to do. For example, if you are okay with hosting sleepovers, then that's a privilege. Think of everything they like to do right now, how much of it they typically do, and whether those activities are in alignment with what you want for them.

This first list of privileges will be baseline motivators and will include everything that you are okay with them doing if they behave moderately well. These will be your Main Rewards. To illustrate, if they currently watch six hours of TV a week, and you are ok with that, six hours of TV would be part of their Main Rewards.

Next, we need to determine what your child would want to do that is NOT part of your typical week. These are the **Major Rewards** – Rewards earned for going just a little above and beyond each week. What would be special for them? Again, these are things they would like that YOU are ready, willing, and able to do. These are going to be the real Rewards – what they are really working towards, so the juicier the better. Think about what would be really special to your kids. You can start small by choosing to add more quantity to your Main Rewards. For example, if six hours of television is part of their Main Rewards, then even allowing them to watch an additional two hours could be special If you have a sleepover as part of the Main Rewards, then maybe having two friends sleepover would be extra special. In these examples, I'm just enhancing the Main Reward.

You can also incorporate other things they like to do that aren't part of a regular week, such as going to the movies, bowling, ice-skating, going out for ice cream or another special dessert. You get the idea. Something extra special, that they would love, that you'd be willing to let them choose within a given week.

And that brings us to **Mega Rewards**. I suggest incorporating what I call "big-ticket" motivators into your Rewards System, as well. This allows you to get your kids to work towards something really amazing, that they can have a few times a year. Mega Rewards are Rewards that you wouldn't necessarily agree to on a weekly basis. For example, my kids can work towards tickets to a live sporting event. That's not something they would do on a regular week, as the tickets are expensive, and the games run late. Another high-ticket Mega Reward in my house is inviting three kids to a sleepover.

To further illustrate, my client Tiffany has two daughters who like to go to shows – musicals, plays, ballets, and such. Getting to attend a local, high school musical – which is relatively inexpensive and simple to attend – is something her family uses as a Major Reward. But they also follow their city's theater productions and select a couple of shows a year that they can attend as a Mega Reward. Theater tickets fall into Mega Rewards because the tickets are more expensive, and the girls like to get new outfits to dress up for the occasion, so it's something the family earns just a few times a year. For Tiffany's family, banking for Mega Rewards has worked very effectively. Her girls are motivated to save up as much as they can for shows and fancy clothes. And because Tiffany *wants to say yes* to the shows, because her girls have *earned it*, she enjoys the shopping trips and going to the shows just as much as her daughters!

So far, we have been talking about identifying the things that motivate your kids that would fall into the five types of Rewards – Micro, Mini, Main, Major, and Mega. And I realize that you don't yet fully understand how the types are related to your currency, your expectations, and the overall system. Not to worry! In the next few paragraphs, I will explain how your kids can use "extra" currency to earn Major Rewards and can "bank" currency for earning Mega Rewards. Then on Day 26, we will put it all together, step by step. The Rewards System isn't in full focus for you just yet, but I promise it's much simpler and easy to implement than it may seem at this moment. Hang in there – we're almost at the finish line!

Alright, let's get back to Major and Mega Rewards! Major Rewards are those that can be used within a regular week if they have earned "extra" currency – currency beyond what they need to earn their Main Reward. If you are also including Mega Rewards in your system, which are earned over periods of time longer than a week, that requires you and your kids to "bank" that extra currency earned. Banking is giving them the option to save any extra Rewards they don't choose to spend that week on Major Rewards to use at some future date on a Mega Reward. I'm going to explain banking for Mega Rewards in its simplest form. Then I will hint at other ways that you might customize your system to best suit YOUR family.

Let's say that you operate on a five-day weekly interval, and your family has three Transitions a day. At the end of a successful week, your child would have 15 units of currency (3 successful Routines times 5 days) required to earn their Main Reward. There are a couple of ways that your kids could earn more than 15 units of currency, giving them "extra" to use toward Major and Mega Rewards.

One way, that I use in my home and highly recommend, is giving them an extra unit of currency for having a "perfect" week. That is, my kids have the opportunity to earn 15 beads for completing their 15 weekly Routines. But every week that they successfully complete all 15 Routines, I throw in an extra bead for having a perfect track record for that week. Therefore, at the end of the week, they have one extra bead to use toward a Major Reward OR that they can "bank" to save up for a Mega Reward.

A second way to earn extra currency is to demonstrate behavior that is "above and beyond" my expectations. For example, if you "catch" your older child helping your younger child with homework without your prompting, they can earn an extra unit of currency to reinforce that behavior. Doing extra "Contributions" (remember those are chores) would be another way that your child could go above and beyond expectations. I hope it goes without saying at this point, but if something like that happens, you need to make your child aware of the how and the why of earning that extra currency. Don't forget to always be "sprinkling" and be making connections for your kids!

So, at the end of the week, if your kids have more currency than is required for earning their Main Reward, they can choose to apply that extra to a Major Reward they can have that week or to bank it to save up for a Mega Reward. In my home, Major Rewards tend to be things my kids can "buy" with one or two extra beads. Mega Rewards, on the other hand, are much more expensive and will cost more currency so your children will need to bank or "save up" to get them.

On Day 26 we will spell out the details of how to align your Routines, currency, and Rewards with your expectations for your child.

One final note on currency before we move on, which will put all the Rewards pieces together for you. Thus far, we have been talking about how your kids will *earn* currency, and you may be wondering if there are reasons to take currency *away* from your child. The answer is "yes," but we have to do so very carefully.

Earlier in the book, I emphasized how The 28-Day Stress-Free Family System strives to focus on good behavior and, therefore, deals with consequences very strategically. We talked about two types of consequences. There are Relevant Consequences, which are those that happen at the moment of the infraction. And there exists the consequence of the *absence* of Rewards. That is, if your kids simply fail to earn enough currency to receive Rewards, that becomes a consequence. For example, if my kids don't earn enough beads during the week, they may not have enough for what they want, but I'm not taking anything away. That's a very important distinction. You will see that they will quickly pick up the benefits of earning their Rewards because this system builds good habits and it *works*.

On the other hand, within the Reward system, there are ways they can lose beads they've already earned this week. This is the part of the Reward system that speaks to the Rhythms, Rules, and expectations around their behavior. Again, the Reward system mainly deals with successful completion of Routines. But let's say you decided that you were only going to say something two times (i.e., it's one of your Rules for Mom), yet the kids are still not listening to you when you speak, even though you're adhering to all the other system guidelines and *Signature Moves*. That is, you've been using The Three Cs (calm, clear, concise directions) and you have been reinforcing the behavior with The TRIBE Method (Time, Recognition, Importance, Benefit, Encouragement). Now, what do you do?

Well, the chance of losing currency in the Reward System is your solution. My *Signature Moves* around losing currency are:

- Use only one or two ways your children can lose currency
- When they do lose currency, they lose it twice as fast as it is earned

We're limiting reasons for losing currency to one or two things because we want to set them up for success – we want to make it easy to earn and hard to lose.

At the same time, we want the loss of currency, when it does occur, to really have an impact on them so that we nip the negative behaviors in the bud.

Let's take an example to illustrate how these two *Signature Moves* make it work.

Mom has a Rule that she will give instructions no more than twice. Therefore, if Mom has to say something a third time, two beads will be lost. Your kids will know that it will take getting through two entire Routines to replace those lost beads – over an infraction that occurred in a matter of minutes or even seconds. So, do you think they will want to lose them over not listening to you when you tell them to do something? No way! And once your kids are earning currency in your Rewards System, they will fully comprehend how much those beads are worth in terms of what they can "buy." They figure out quickly that it's totally not worth it to make Mom repeat herself!

Using this method takes care of ALL the Rules and the Rhythms in your home. Any time your kids are in danger of fouling up a Rule or Rhythm, simply state what you would like to happen. If you have to, repeat the instruction, hold up two fingers as a warning that you are saying it the second time. If they still don't comply, they lose two beads. They'll pick this up very quickly and you will not have to keep repeating yourself! See the magic in that? "Making Mom repeat herself" is ONE way to lose currency, but it covers nearly EVERY problem that can occur!

Of course, you'll need to determine which infractions would warrant the loss of beads, but I strongly suggest that you stick to just one or two infractions. You need to make these count! I suggest choosing the one or two things that you tend to grapple with most in your home. Think of the two things that, if you eliminated them, would make the biggest impact on your home. You have to weigh these carefully. If it's too easy to lose a bead, they'll get frustrated and won't work so hard to earn the currency, so make sure it's something worthy. Consider the common infractions in your home – the ones that make you the craziest – as well as your values-based Rules as you decide the one or two things that can result in a loss of a unit of currency.

You'll need to figure out your Main Rewards and some special Major Rewards – these are your children's motivators! Think of as many as possible. You want them to be able to shop a menu of options. Decide whether or not you want to offer some big-ticket motivators and allow them to bank for Mega Rewards. Lastly, decide on the one or two infractions where they would lose their hard-earned beads.

Wow, we covered a lot! We are almost done with the pieces of the Reward System, and then I'm going to go through my kid's Rewards System and show you how all the pieces fit together!

Day 25 Assignment:

- Routines & Rhythms – Keep "sprinkling" and "TRIBE'ing"
- Rules!
  o Keep declaring your Rules for Mom into the mirror each day. Research shows that it takes at least 21 days (though some argue that it requires 66 days) to form a new habit.
- Rewards!
  o Create a master list of Rewards your children can earn for each type of Rewards – Micro, Mini, Main, Major, and Mega.
    - Remember that you may not need Micro and Mini Rewards in your home and that you may decide not to use Mega Rewards. But everyone must have Main and Major Rewards for your kids for the Rewards System to work properly!
    - Think of as many as possible. You want your kids to be able to select from a "menu" of options.
    - Note that you're still keeping this a secret for now. When we get to Day 28, your child will have the opportunity to give input into what Rewards they will want to motivate them!

Day 26:
Pillar 4 Rewards – Attainable Expectations for Rewards

Today's Overview

- Signature Moves
    - o Five Levels of Rewards
    - o Setting an achievable baseline for Main Rewards
    - o Establishing "bonus" behaviors

"Acknowledge and voice the positives LOUDER than the negatives."

~Tanya Masse, aka Comic Strip Mama, mom, wife, author, blogger, cartoonist

We have spelled out most of the Rewards System, and now we're ready to finish going over the parts and put it all together! Today, we're going to finalize the Rewards System and currency by aligning your expectations with your child's abilities.

To do this, you must consider each of your children carefully. Now that you've had several weeks since you've rolled out your Routines, what are realistic expectations for your kids to successfully complete those Routines? Begin by thinking of the bare minimum that is both realistic for your kids and at a level that you would find acceptable. Assign that attainable, acceptable level a percentage. For example, if your child is currently, correctly completing their Routines 70%

of the time, then the bare minimum that you would accept would probably be 50%.   Meaning that you know they will be able to, at least, consistently complete their Routines 50% of the time.

This percentage is not the ultimate goal, as we are working toward 100%. This percentage I'm asking you to come up with is your *baseline*. And the baseline is based on where they are *right now*. It's merely the bare minimum you expect. The bare minimum you will accept must be lower than they are currently performing because it must be attainable every week. We want them to have low-level benchmarks so that they can feel successful and so that they are always able to earn and enjoy the Main Rewards. We want to make sure that our kids are always able to have a minimum level of Rewards.

Another *Signature Move* is beginning with easy successes. We start by Rewarding them for what they are already able to do and build from there. Allowing our kids to be successful early on in The System is one of the things that makes The System work. When the kids are "winning" right out of the gate, they are motivated to keep going and do even better. That's why setting this bare minimum percentage is important. The Reward System is designed to help them exceed your expectations, but we have to start where they are, with a minimum expectation.

Once you've determined your bare minimum expectation, think about what you consider to be bonus territory. We want to give them lots of opportunities to earn extra beads for going above and beyond. It bears repeating yet again: The Reward system revolves primarily around Routines, Rhythms, and Rules. They earn beads for successful completion of their Routines throughout the day. Your kids also have ONE or two ways to lose beads – when Mom has to give them an instruction more than two times or for another infraction which you have chosen. On the flip side, we want to offer them MANY ways to EARN bonus beads. To do that, we add in the areas where we want our kids to improve that don't have to do with Routines, Rhythms or Rules. So, consider what areas you would like them to improve.

The Rewards System works because it's heavily weighted toward positive behavior and an abundance of Rewards! This is where it gets fun. I love talking about bonus territory!

Let's look at some examples. Maybe you'd like your child to raise their grades at school. If they're currently bringing home grades in the 80's, bonus territory could be defined as 90 or above. Or, let's say your child has been exceptionally helpful or has done an extra Contribution (chore). Bonus territory involves any extra opportunities for your kids to earn. Think of any areas that require improvement or areas that are extra difficult for them to tackle. Include these as items that warrant bonus currency.

Technically, Rewards need to be tied to very specific, defined behaviors, but I do suggest Rewarding excellent behavior. Every once in a while, if they're just doing such an amazing job helping each other out, or taking initiative, or making your life really easy in some way, you can decide to give them an extra, discretionary bead. Please note that this doesn't mean that *every* time they do something nice they need to be Rewarded with more currency. You want them to do nice things because they like to do nice things, not because they're being Rewarded. Again, we're fine-tuning their inner guidance systems. Therefore, in my home, the kids don't know when I'll Reward them with extra currency, so they just need to do good things because they want to do good things. When I catch them performing random acts of kindness or taking the initiative and being super helpful, I decide in the moment. At other times, I simply use my "sprinkling" and TRIBE to encourage my kids and reinforce their good behavior.

So, try to think of as many ways as possible to be able to Reward your child for bonus territory behavior. Imagine how happy you would be if your child brought home two 90%s on their report card and was super helpful in the morning after completing their Routines. Wouldn't you be so happy to give them extra beads, so you can pile the Rewards on? Wouldn't that be your greatest pleasure? And can you imagine how much better your child will behave after having so much fun spending their beads on Rewards?

Tomorrow is the final day on Rewards when we will be assigning value to the currency you've chosen, as well as the value of items on the Major and Mega Rewards menus.

For now, let's just give two examples of how the currency and your expectation percentage works with your week and the Main Reward.

Natalie, a mom who completed my 28-Day Stress-Free Family online program, has a son who was in kindergarten when she implemented the system in her house. Because he was younger, she determined that her son needed Micro Rewards at each Transition, which took the form of iPad time or reading a book with Mom. By the time she got to the Rewards Pillar, her son, with a little help from her, was successfully completing his Morning and Afternoon Routines. His Evening Routine remained a little challenging, but they were working on it. So, she decided that her baseline percent was 50%. That is, even though he was successfully completing two out of three Transitions each day, she set the bare minimum a bit lower. This way, she knows that every week he will have that opportunity to be successful and earn Main Rewards. She chose small blocks as his form of currency. As those blocks piled up, he became more and more motivated to complete all of his Routines successfully. He was successful 10 out of 15 times, but she decided that she would set the bare minimum at only 8 (roughly 50%). That way, every week, they both know he would be able to earn the Main Reward. See? Because Natalie knew her son would be successful 10 times a week, she set the baseline at 8 times so that each week he could feel successful and enjoy The Main Rewards and have a surplus that he could spend towards Major Rewards.

On the other end of the spectrum, my client Myra had 12-year-old twins when she rolled out The 28-Day Stress-Free Family System. By the time she added Rewards, they had been several weeks into practicing their Routines. They were older and very capable. After just a few weeks of practice under their belts, her kids rarely failed to complete their Routines. They operated on a five-day, four-Transition week, due to their afterschool activities. The maximum number of units of currency they could earn for weekly Routines was 20 (5 Days times 4 Routines). She noted that they picked up on the Routines very quickly and would likely earn 19 or 20 beads most weeks. Myra decided to set the bare minimum at 15 beads for earning the Main Reward. This way, she ensured that they would always have, at least, Main Rewards and would likely earn a surplus of 4 or 5 extra beads a week to spend on Major Rewards.

Is it starting to make sense now? Tomorrow, we will put all the final pieces in place for Rewards, and then we get to plan how to roll out the entire system for your family!

Day 26 Assignment:

- Routines & Rhythms – Do I even need to tell you?

- Rules – Keep declaring your Rules for Mom into the mirror. I promise this won't go on forever but sticking with it now will pay dividends.

- Rewards!

  o Come up with your minimum percentage and/or units of currency for your baseline. This will determine the minimum requirement for earning Main Rewards.

  o Brainstorm as many positive behaviors as possible that put your kids in "bonus" currency territory.

Day 27:
Pillar 4 Rewards – Putting It All Together

Today's Overview

- Signature Moves
    - o A menu of Rewards options
    - o Assigning value to currency and Rewards
    - o "Command Central"
- What you'll need
    - o Your journal
    - o Currency and containers for tomorrow
    - o Large dry erase board (or similar) for your Command Central Rewards Board
    - o Smaller dry erase board (or similar) for your Rules Board

---

"It is only through raising expectations and striving for excellence that our children can reach their full potential."

~Brad Henry, American lawyer and former governor of Oklahoma

Okay, here's where it all comes together! Remember you still haven't shared any of this with your kids. That's up next in Pillar 5, Revolutionize. When you get to Revolutionize, I will walk you through how to have a family meeting to introduce the big picture to your kids. In doing so, you will ask for their input, so they will have the opportunity to contribute to The System. And during that meeting, you may get some fabulous ideas about Rules, Rhythms, and Rewards that you add to The System. However, you are going to have the vast majority of it figured out ahead of time! You're just not going to let on that you already have a master plan. By doing the legwork ahead of time, you know you'll have a rock-solid plan ready to roll out to them. But by also asking for their input, you will bc allowing them some ownership over the system. Having ownership increases their buy-in of the system, which makes them more likely to comply with your expectations!

So, in this chapter, you will be finalizing your master plan. I think the easiest way for me to clarify how the entire Rewards System is managed is to walk you through how I execute The System in my home. You can then tweak it to accommodate The System you have been creating, tailored to your family's specific needs.

To finalize Rewards, you will need a large dry erase board where you will to write out your system when you Revolutionize and have your family meeting. The dry erase board represents my *Signature Move* I call "Command Central." I use a single, large white dry erase board for Command Central because I have one system for all three of my children. The board lives by their Tomorrow Boxes, at the door where my children enter and exit, so they see it daily, coming and going. You could elect to use a single big white board like I do, or a couple of smaller ones, one for each child. I like the dry erase board because it allows me to easily make changes and updates as they grow. If a large whiteboard is impractical for your family, you could use a large poster board or something similar.

At this point in the game, you need to map out what will be on your Command Central, but you are not yet creating your actual board. That is, you need to know what you want to appear on your board, but you won't actually create the board until Revolutionize. You will write out everything for your family's Command Central "live," during your family meeting in Revolutionize. I know this may all be slightly confusing right now but stay with me. I will walk you through everything, one step at a time!

Command Central:

Command Central will be divided into four quadrants. On the top left, you'll write out the bare minimum you decided on. My kids have three Transitions a day and get rewarded one bead for each Transition, which means they have 15 opportunities to earn beads for Transitions. My kids have been working this Rewards System forever, so it's very reasonable to expect them to successfully complete their Morning, Afternoon and Evening Routines, plus their Contributions (chores) during the week at least 12 out of the 15 times. So, 12 is the bare minimum behavior which will get them their Main Rewards. (Again, I set the bare minimum at a level a bit lower than I know they will achieve, ensuring that they are always awarded their Main Rewards)

When my kids have a "perfect" week and earn all 15 of the potential beads, I throw in the extra bead for this good track record. That's because sometimes, the whole is greater than the sum of its parts. I want them to have a really great week and to want to work hard to get through it without a single hiccup. So, a perfect week means an extra bead. When we get to spending, you'll see that the extra bead is worth a lot, which makes it worth it for them to strive for that perfect week. Remember, I want them to be successful, I want to set the bar low enough that they can reasonably meet expectations every week, and then I ramp up the ante for big fun. I also have my kids do 15 minutes of Contributions a day as part of their bare minimum.

To recap, 12 is the bare minimum for Main Rewards, which means anything over 12 is bonus territory. Therefore, the top, left corner of my Command Central dry erase board in my home is spelled out like this:

3 Routines X 5 days = 15 *[Includes 15 minutes of Contributions Every day]*

A "perfect" week of 15 earns an extra bead = 16 *[Over 12 beads = Major or Mega Rewards]*

This means they get to spend any beads earned over 12 on Major or Mega Rewards. In this scenario, they have 4 extra beads to spend. (16-12=4)

If you will be operating on a seven-day week, with three Routines per day, the top of your first column might look like this

3 Routines X 7 days = 21 *[Includes 15 minutes of Contributions Every day]*

A "perfect" 21 earns an extra bead = 22 *[Over 17 beads = Major or Mega Rewards]*

This means they get to spend any beads earned over 17. In this scenario, they have 5 extra beads to spend. (22-17=5)

On the bottom left quadrant, I have the Main Rewards spelled out – what they earn for achieving the minimum of 12 beads. And because the bare minimum is set LOWER than your child is able to perform, this means they ALWAYS get these privileges. So, every week they, at the very least, they get to enjoy the Main Rewards.   In my house, it looks like this:

- One hour each weekend day of screen time (TV or video games)
- One televised sports game to watch over the weekend (above and beyond TV/video game time)
- Two television shows midweek
- Twenty minutes of free time each weekday night

Are you thinking "What? That's it?!" Yep, that's the baseline! But hold the phone! You have to keep a couple of things in mind. Remember, that this is the bare minimum. If my kids only earned 12 beads for the week, that would mean they had a really challenging week – NOT a good week for us at all. Secondly, I keep them super busy with sports all weekend, when they aren't playing an organized game, they're shooting hoops in a court, taking swings in a batting cage, or doing their homework. They actually don't have that much extra time– they probably only have about three or four extra hours on the weekend anyway. Plus, if they had a week where they only earned the *bare minimum*, I want them to be bored. I want them to be motivated do better next time, right?

Let's keep going! With the bare minimum at 12, but the opportunity to earn 16 beads, my kids would already start the weekend with a surplus of 4 beads. Remember, anything above the minimum currency is a bonus, and my kids have the opportunity each week to earn 4 bonus beads *just* for successfully completing their Routines. Soon, we'll talk about what the bonus currency can buy them.

In the top right quadrant, I have spelled out the ways that my kids can earn additional beads for behavior beyond what's required from their Routines, as well as what bonus beads can "buy."

In my house, they can add a bead by earning over a 90 on their tests. I noticed that they were coming home with grades in the low 90s, which made me think they could push a bit more and get over 95%. So, I added an extra bead for a 95% to give them the incentive for pushing themselves just a little harder. And guess what happened next? Yep! They started bringing home test scores over 95%! Now they earn two beads for every test over 95.

If your child brings home test scores in the low 80s, consider allowing them to earn an extra bead for an 85% and another for scores over 87%! See how this works? You just move the bar a little bit higher than what they are doing now.

If I catch my kids exhibiting exceptional behavior, which is something I decide, I sometimes give them an extra bead.   Like I said before, sometimes, not always. I'm deliberately inconsistent with it because I don't want them behaving well only for the bead. Most of the time, I use TRIBE for recognizing exceptional behavior. But sometimes, I give them an extra bead. Here is why. MOM is the one who decides, right? We don't want to raise kids who say, "See mom? I helped you pack up lunch, what do I get for that?" Right? You want them to be internally motivated to be exceptional people.

There's one more thing I'd like to add to this topic. When your home is running smoothly, and your Routines are on track, when your mornings are easy, and your kids go to bed happy and on time, you will be absolutely surprised at how many opportunities there are to bonus your kids for excellent behavior. They will just all around behave better more often. So even though it's bonus territory, my kids end up getting at least one bead for exceptional behavior every week. That means I've caught them behaving exceptionally several times. That's what's about to happen in your home. Aren't you getting excited? Can you see how easily your child will be able to rack up those beads?

Underneath the ways bonus beads can be earned, the board includes the Major and Mega Rewards that bonus beads can be used for, as well as how much those items "cost."

The top right quadrant of my command central looks like this:

Bonus beads

1 = 90+ on tests

1 = 95+ on tests

1 = Exceptional behavior (I decide)

1 = Extra Contribution

The final quadrant, on the bottom right, details all the ways they can "spend" their bonus currency. In my house, it looks like this:

Major Rewards Currency

1 = Sleepover

1 = Movie

1 = Special Dessert

1 = Pizza Night

2 = School night televised sports game

2 = School Night Xbox hour

2 = School Night TV

Mega Rewards Currency

10 = Sporting event

10 = Three-friend sleepover

One final note on the value of the currency in my house. If you look at the list of things they can "buy" under Major Rewards, the cost is one bead if they want to do it over the weekend. But sometimes, when everything is in order, and we have the time, I allow them to "buy" a Major Reward during the week. However, the cost of the item doubles on weekdays. So, for example, if one of my sons has completed his Routines and his homework, he's bringing home good grades and so forth, he can decide to use *two* of his beads to watch extra Television on a school night. I doubled the value of a school night privilege because I don't want them to do it all the time, and I want to keep it special. Doubling the value makes it harder for them to spend it so it's an easy way to slow down how often they can do it. There are many ways to customize your Rewards System to suit your family. This is one of the ways that you could decide to tailor your system to allow for more fun. No two families Command Central boards are alike. Feel free to tweak the systems to suit your family's needs. As long as you stay within the overall framework and guidelines, it will work like a charm!

Since the Rewards System is centered around the positive – lots of ways to *earn* Rewards – add that as a heading on the Command Central board. But we also want our kids to keep in mind that they can lose beads – and to remember how costly it is.

This is what that will look like. If they're about to lose two beads, I remind them of the expectation. For example, if I direct one of my kids to fold laundry for their 15 minutes of Contribution, and he responds with, "Mom, why do I have to do that?" I will give him one more chance, to say something along the lines of "Sure, Mom." I'll instruct him just one more time and that's it. Because one of my Rules for Mom is "I will not be a nag," and that means I will give an instruction up to two times *only*. My kids know I'm not going to say it a third time. Also, it's the one way they can lose beads! And losing can be FAST. Since they earn one bead at a time but can lose two for a single infraction, they quickly learn that it is not worth it.

Your child will quickly learn how this system works and you will see that you rarely have to take away a bead. I can't remember the last time I had to do that! Spending beads in this system is so much fun that losing two beads is a big deal! After your kids lose currency once or twice, you'll be done with that for good!

Here's a table to illustrate where each component of the Rewards System will appear on your Command Central Board.

REWARDS! So many ways to earn!	
Bare Minimum Requirements for Routines	Ways to Earn Bonus beads
Main Rewards for Meeting Bare Minimum	Bead Currency Major & Mega Rewards
Just ONE way to lose – Lose 2 beads if Mom has to tell you something more than twice	

Sketch out in your journal what you intend to write on your board. But don't write the items on the actual board until tomorrow. You'll write everything on the board while holding the family meeting with your kids!

Day 27 Assignment:

- Routines & Rhythms – Only do the bare minimum with prompts and reminders to keep them on track. Allow them to become more and more independent but keep striving toward making them successful. Their success is going to be critically important now that we are about to unveil the whole system and incorporate Rewards. This system works because you have already set them up for success, and now you and they are going to have fun as they get to reap the Rewards of that success!

- Rules – Declare them, sister!

- Rewards!

    o Sketch out in your journal or on a blank sheet of paper, what the quadrants of your Command Central board are going to look like.

- Notate the bare minimum expectation and what Main Rewards your child would receive for performing the bare minimum.

- Record what they would earn for meeting the bare minimum/Main Reward.

- Decide the additional ways they can earn a bonus bead (e.g., test scores).

- Make a list of the Major and Mega Rewards they can "buy" with their bonus beads.

Day 28:
Pillar 5
REVOLUTIONIZE
– Transform Your Home

Today's Overview:

- Signature Moves
  - o The *Magic* of a Complete and Integrated System
  - o Kicking off the System with a family meeting
  - o Getting input and buy-in from your kids

"Let us make our future now, and let us make our dreams tomorrow's reality."

~Malala Yousafzai, Pakistani activist for female education and the youngest Nobel Prize laureate

Woo-hoo! We are in the last Pillar, Revolutionize! This Pillar is where it all comes together for your family. And you'll finally be letting them in on everything you've been working on so far. At least sort of! That is, you're going to have a family meeting where you discuss and ask for input on the Rules and Rewards, but you're still not letting on that you have been planning this all along.

Now you know that the secret to removing all the stress and chaos from your house is having **a** SYSTEM! Your system is going to transform your home into one that is calm, peaceful, and stress-free. One of the biggest problems I see with moms struggling at home is that they don't understand they need a complete system, with all the parts working together in order to remove the stress from their home. Think about the parts of a car on an assembly line - the car isn't assembled UNTIL each part is completed independently, right? First, they make sure each part works correctly and then they put the parts together. Otherwise, the car wouldn't run, right? Well, it's the same thing with your home, you want it running just like a well-oiled machine. Does this make sense?

One of the other problems I see with moms struggling at home is that they may know they need a system, but they think it's going to be hard or complicated to do. Or they're afraid it will turn them into a mean mom because systems don't really sound fun, right? But now you know how easy it is! And let me just say that, when I was scrambling all the time, when my home was in chaos, when I was nagging at my kids all the time, my patience was running really thin. And because my patience was running so thin, I was yelling a lot. And my answer to a lot of things, was NO. And lots of times, the answer was NO because I didn't have the energy to do something, or I was just too stressed. Actually, I *was* a mean mom. Putting a system in place allowed me to be NICER. I've said it before but it's worth repeating: There's so much more room for fun when your home is running smoothly, and your kids are behaving well. Right? It's much easier to say 'yes' when everything is just humming and relaxed, yes? In reality, putting a system in place allowed me to be the fun mom. And one of the things I love about my system is the *Signature Move* of working on one part, getting it working correctly and then moving on to the next part. So, what we did so far was systematically decrease the stress at home by making sure each part functioned independently. In Revolutionize, we integrate them. We put them all together with your family so that it runs like that well-oiled machine.

One last thing before we get into how to Revolutionize with your family meeting, I want to check in with you on what we've done so far. It is essential that you have read Days 1-27 *and* completed the assignments *and* you have been implementing and practicing the Routines and Rhythms, as well as speaking your Rules to yourself and sticking with them. Your kids must be performing their Routines pretty easily by the time you are ready to sit them down with you for a family meeting and get their buy-in. Do not schedule and plan your meeting until you are already seeing a big difference in your house. Your journal should be filled with your assignments where you detailed what you want your home's Rules to be and how you will be structuring your Rewards system.

Also, you need to have all of your supplies ready. Did you select your currency? Do you have all the containers you need for your currency? You need one container to keep your supply of the currency, as well as one container per child where you will "pay" them. If you have small children and you plan to do Micro or Mini Rewards, you may also want to have a second container to hold the currency just for "today."

In addition, you need to have dry erase boards to write down your Rules and Rewards System during your meeting, as well as to hang or lean somewhere in your home so everyone can see them all the time. This is going to be Command Central. I use one large dry erase board for the Rewards System and a smaller one for our Rules. The dry erase boards are ideal because you can easily revise during the meeting by wiping it off, as well as update it when something in your home changes. For example, your kids will find different things they will want to be Rewarded with as they grow up.

If whiteboards aren't practical for your home, I know you can come up with an alternative plan. You're savvy like that! For example, poster boards are inexpensive, plus they're light and easy to move around. The drawback, of course, is that you'll need a new one every time something changes. So, if you do go with something like a poster board, maybe pick up a few so that you can create a rough draft during your meeting and then create a tidier, final version once you and your family have settled all the details.

Again, if you've been following along with me, then everything should be in place and you're ready to move forward with the family meeting to Revolutionize your home. If you haven't kept up with everything or if you've missed a step, now is the time to go back. As I mentioned in the Rewards part of the book, your kids need to be succeeding *before the meeting,* in order for the family meeting to have its Revolutionary effects. So, if you haven't been practicing your Routines enough and therefore your children are NOT easily meeting your bare minimum requirement, take the time now to help them. If you need another week or two to nail it down, I'd rather you take time now and start off on the right foot. In the grand scheme of things, another two weeks is nothing. It's much more important to do this *right* than it is to do it *quickly!* I want nothing more than for you and your kids to have great success with this System, so don't rush into Revolutionize if you're not ready. This is not a race!

If you're not ready, take that week or two to help your kids get everything down pat, and then come back to this point in the book. I'll wait here.

Okay, you are ready to Revolutionize! I am going to share with you what you need to run an effective family meeting to get your kids on board. Please read through all of today *and* Day 28 *before* you have your meeting. Conducting your meeting is not at all difficult, but it is a little nuanced. You will want to make sure you understand the complete process and let it sink in before you begin to Revolutionize.

If you're wondering *why* it's so important to have this sit down and get their buy-in, I want to ensure you understand the magic of this

Pillar. I mean, you *could* just keep practicing your Routines and Rhythms, casually inform them you'll start Rewarding them and just keep plugging along without having a formal meeting.   You're definitely seeing improvement in your home already, right? So, you could just stop there.

But if you did stop, you'd miss out on the *magic* of *integrating* all the Pillars. Two elements MUST be in place for your System to truly be effective. The steps must be *complete,* and they must be *integrated.* We've been working all along on completing the steps. Revolutionize is what integrates them. Plus, bringing your kids in on it and having them "help" you create The System is the secret sauce, the *Signature Move.* Integrating with the kids' help is the part that turns your home into a well-oiled machine. All the parts will work seamlessly together, with your children *wanting* to do it!

Now, if you've never had a family meeting before, don't worry! I have your back, and I'm going to set you up for success. And if your family does already have family meetings, know that your Revolutionize meeting is NOT like your regular family meeting. It's different because, in Revolutionize, you are scrapping the old systems you may have had running in your home and/or introducing your new system. Allow me to give you the 10,000-foot view of what Revolutionize will look like.

You will be involving your kids in creating The System, giving them a lot of say in how it will work, as well as opportunities to make decisions. In essence, you're giving them the *power* to choose how they want to live. What they DON'T know, is that you've been planting seeds all along! Plus, during your Revolutionize meeting, you'll be guiding and prompting them with your words. They will naturally be led to the conclusion that what they want is The Stress-Free Family System that you already created. You *will* be asking for their input and tweaking what you have created to incorporate their ideas. But those will be minor changes. By holding the meeting, you will be making it appear that it was virtually all their idea!

And if that seems underhanded to you or makes you uncomfortable because you're "tricking" them, think of it like this: If you took them to see a magician, would you be upset at the magician's use of sleight of hand to pull off the tricks? Of course not, because even if your kids are old enough to know it's not "real" magic, they're still *delighted* by the magician's tricks, right? It's like that. You're just using a bit of Mom magic to delight your kids with this System that they will appreciate as much as you will!

Before I give you the Revolutionize meeting process, I want to offer a few pro tips – some more *Signature Moves!*

- As I mentioned above, ensure you have your supplies:
  o Your kids' Routines checklists
  o Their Tomorrow Boxes (if it's convenient to have them in your meeting space)
  o Currency
  o Currency bowls or other containers
  o Two dry erase boards (or alternative), one for Rules and one for Rewards.
    ▪ You know at least 90% of what is going on those boards, but you start the meeting with blank boards and "build" them out with your kids.
- Plan ahead to have some sort of *celebration* right after the meeting. Pick something that will seem celebratory to your kids, whatever that might be. Going out for ice cream or another favorite treat is always a winner but pick something that will light *them* up.
- Be genuine but also be enthusiastic. You should be excited about this process, and you want it to be contagious!

- Be as open-minded as possible to your kids' suggestions, but only incorporate what *you* can live with – and therefore stick to.

- Ideally, wait to have your Revolutionize meeting until Sunday afternoon.. So, if you are reading this on a Monday, just use the extra days to make sure that the Routines, Rhytms, and Rules are nailed down and wait until Sunday to have your meeting.

  o This works best because whether you are using a five-day or seven-day payout schedule, the week kicks off on Sunday evening. So, you can have your meeting and start that night.

  o Everyone, even small children, associate Monday with a fresh start. (How many people do you know who've started a diet on Thursday? None, right?!)

  o Jot down some phrases you can use when your kids suggest something that throws you for a loop (e.g.., "Let's go on an African safari for a Reward!"). Personally, I like, *"Hmm. That's interesting. Let me think about that, but for now...."*

- Keep your meeting short and sweet. Also, the younger the child, the shorter your meeting needs to be.

Whew, that's a long list! But all the items are simple and clear and will set you up for the best possible results from your meeting!

Now I'm going to give you the gist of conducting your family's Revolutionize meeting. As I hinted above, your homework will be to prepare the things you know you want to say, as you explain how The System works, as well as to develop those few, key phrases that will help you as they give their input. Therefore, you may want to jot down some notes in your journal about things you want to be sure to say at your meeting, as you read through the process. For simplicity, I'm going to refer to beads anywhere you will be using or talking about your currency.

Come to the meeting prepared with your Routines, Rhythms, Rules, and Rewards already written out in your notes. Tell your kids that you've been thinking about how well things are going, so you want to start Rewarding them for their good behavior.

Then begin to go through the System in order, just like we did – Routines, Rhythms, and Rules – but instead of *telling* them, you're asking them for their input on each part.

Ask them what they think would be good Rules for your home. Guide them to the Rules that you have developed and write your and their ideas on your Rules board.

Go through each portion of your Command Central board and record what you discuss:

- The bare minimum requirements for Routines and the beads they'll earn
- What they receive as Main Rewards for meeting the bare minimum
- How easy it will be to earn additional beads – Ask them to tell you how they will want to spend their beads.
- Ask them what Rewards they would like when they have earned Major and Mega Rewards.
- Decide and Record the currency it will "cost" for each Reward next to each item on the board.

As you do this, you're basically guiding them to the answers you've already mapped out but be open-minded to what they have to say. It's possible that they'll come up with suggestions you hadn't considered, but you are okay with.

And that's it! *You are ready!* And you'll find that the meeting is actually fun! I will warn you that you need to be prepared for the unexpected – because *something* unexpected is *going* to happen. You know, "kids say the darnedest things."

Be open-minded about Rules and Rewards that they suggest. They will most certainly come up with some great ideas that you didn't think of. Incorporate those into your System. On the flip side, don't be surprised if they say something that catches you completely off guard.

For example, when I had our first family meeting with the boys, everything was going great. When I asked them what Rules we should have, every one of them offered Rules I'd had in mind: no shouting, listen when someone else is talking and don't interrupt, clean up after yourself, etc. The meeting was rolling so nicely and easily. All of a sudden, my youngest one suggested the Rule "no spitting on each other." I had to stop myself from laughing out loud! Obviously, I didn't want them spitting on each other, But I had never seen them do that, and I had no idea that was even on their radar! The funny thing is that they were *all in agreement* that "no spitting" was a good rule And because I wanted them to feel like they were contributing to the Rules of the house, guess what went on the Rules board? No spitting! Now that they're so much older, we still laugh about the story!

So, just roll with your meeting, enjoy your kids, and have fun with it! And remember, your whole world is about to have lots more room for family fun! And that's because....

The integration of The System truly begins when you get to Rewards. This is SO important! If you don't integrate these parts, you won't have the success that you want. The success you *deserve!* The basic idea is that they will earn Rewards based on their successful completion of the Routines, Rhythms, and Rules. You've set your base level of Rewards low enough to achieve, so they will be successful and feel encouraged. You can emphasize how easy it's going to be for them to attain their Rewards. But you've also set some higher standards so that they work hard to reap the larger Rewards. Again, they should feel excited about how clear and simple it's going to be for them to earn Rewards that *they* chose to put on your list.

And this is the most important thing: They must believe that THEY are the ones creating the Rewards System based on Routines, Rhythms and Rules THAT THEY just helped YOU create. Remember, you're just guiding them to YOUR answers. But they're going to think they came up with the whole idea, which is what you WANT. They're much more likely to follow a system they created, right? And that's the bird's eye view of how we integrate the parts and get them on board! In a nutshell, The Rewards System takes their Routines, Rhythms, and Rules into account. Revolutionize is your family meeting and the implementation and execution of the system.

Day 28 Assignment:

- Routines, Rhythms, and Rules – Keep it all going. Feel free to stay in a "holding pattern" with these first three Pillars if your family doesn't quite have them down pat. You can certainly start preparing yourself for your Revolutionize meeting while you continue to practice. But don't have the meeting until your kids are already being successful. You want the first week of Rewards to knock their socks off – that's what really integrates the whole System and makes it stick!

- Rewards – Keep practicing Relevant Consequences for infractions and TRIBE for good behavior!

- Revolutionize!
  - o Review everything you've created for the first four Pillars (Routines, Rhythms, Rules, Rewards), and sketch out what you want your Command Central and Rules boards to look like after your meeting with your kids.

o Use the guidelines above to plan out your main points and how you'll present them at your family's Revolutionize meeting.

o Host your family's meeting!

Day 29 and Beyond
- Calm and Stress-free

*"Let us not settle for what is simply 'OK' when we have full information on
what can create lasting change."*

Rinku Sen, Indian-American author, and racial activist

I'm so excited for you! After holding your family meeting yesterday, you're entering your first full week of Rewards. So, brace yourself for the Revolution of calm, order, and fun that's about to begin in your home! I can't wait for you to get to the end of this week when you and your kids count the accrued currency. They'll have so much fun "spending" on their Rewards, and it will be so great for you to be able to say "Yes, yes, YES," because your kids will have earned it!

And it will keep getting better and better, week after week. I can testify to that! In fact, your kids will love spending their huge surplus of beads each week. And you'll get to experience one of my favorite feelings in the world: saying "YES" to your kids because they've done such a great job all week and behaved so well. It really is one of the best feelings in the world to happily tell your kids "yes," especially after coming from a place where all your "yeses" were the result of being worn down and exhausted. I'm so excited for you to experience this for yourself.

Once you get a few weeks under your belt, everything is going to begin to happen on autopilot. But for the next month or so, you are going to want to "Sprinkle" like crazy.

- Sprinkle in reminders about how they can lose Rewards quickly by not adhering to Routines, Rhythms, and Rules. (Of course, you will remind them up to two times)
- Sprinkle in that the Routines, Rules, and Rewards that you came up with TOGETHER, as a FAMILY are simple to follow.
- Sprinkle in how much control THEY have over their Rewards and their free time.

"Wow, counting up these beads is so much fun! I love that you got an 87% on that test this week. How are you going to spend those two extra beads?"

"Whoa! Those beads are really adding up. Thanks for helping by folding the clothes. You'll have enough beads to go to that basketball game soon!"

"Way to help your sister gather her things for tomorrow. You're getting a bonus bead for that! That's worth another hour of television for you."

Sprinkle, sprinkle, sprinkle!

Make sure that every time they get a bead, you let them know. They'll be waiting to hear the sound of the bead hit the bowl or to see you write the check mark on their board. Make a big deal out of figuring out how they are going to spend their beads and select Rewards.

When you see them working extra hard, throw them that extra bead. Once in a while, surprise them with a bonus treat by doing something like announcing that you're taking them to the movies or another activity after dinner. A mid-week movie that won't even cost them any beads is a huge deal. When your kids are behaving really well, their grades are great, and your house is calm, you'll see that it's very easy to be generous! Let them reap the Rewards.

Now that your Stress-Free Family System is officially underway, to *keep* your well-oiled machine functioning properly, you need to manage it by consistently inspecting their progress and doling out their beads and Rewards. Your children understand that the System is holding them accountable, and they are expecting you to check up on them.

Think about it. If your child is at least school age, they already "get" accountability. They're given a task, and someone checks it. The teacher assigns them homework and then it gets graded. They're asked to study for tests and the teacher checks them. It's the same concept.

It's critical to the success of your System. In the beginning, it will require more effort on your part, because you want it to be clear to them that you are checking. It's important they understand that you are on top of it and their Rewards are dependent on the inspection. Remember, you need to be obvious with the doling out of the currency.

For me, I drop the bead nice and loud into the bowl as they head out in the morning, and as they walk past me in the afternoon with their Tomorrow Box in their hands. At bedtime, I tell them I'm on my way to add the bead. Whenever your interval is, let them know they've earned their "bead." At the end of the payout cycle, sit down with them and make a big deal of counting up those beads. Talk about spending the beads, saving the beads, what they can do with their beads, all the different options they have, and so on.

For the next few weeks, you might need to inspect at every step within a Routine, then later move to just checking at Transitions and give them their bead. After all these years, I obviously don't need to check my kids at every step or even at each Transition. But I still do check the Transitions. I do it anyway because it keeps me consistent and it keeps them consistent. It keeps my family on track. It takes 20 seconds to do it and reminds us all that we have a System that *works*. So, I peek into their room and their bathroom and give a check into their Tomorrow Box. Rarely do I find something amiss in their room or left out of their Tomorrow Boxes. Everything is linked together and completely, habitually Routine. (In fact, when my kids forget a task or an item for their Tomorrow Box, it's my first sign that they're coming down with something and I may need to take them to the doctor. I consider it a bonus, early-warning System!)

Do you remember I shared with you how chaotic my life was before my Stress-Free Family journey? After dropping my kids off at three different schools, I used to spend a few hours *almost daily* going back home to grab all the things they forgot – lunch, homework, jackets, uniforms – and then make a second trip to their schools, walk into the office, YET AGAIN, and bring my kids their stuff. Can you imagine how embarrassing it was to walk into those school offices several times a week with my kids' stuff? "Yup, it's me! I'm back because he forgot his lunch again." Embarrassing, right? Now it's so nice to think back to that time and realize how far we've come. Isn't that amazing? And that's actually how I started teaching this system! It was such a dramatic change for my family and my kids that when the system started to kick in, EVERYBODY noticed! And moms wanted to know what my secret was.

Unlike the day when I *looked* together but was wearing two different shoes, I *became* "together" and had a secret worth sharing.

And now YOU know what my secret is, too!

Congratulations, I've Got Your Back

Bravo! Congratulations! I am so proud of you and so excited for you! I'd love to be able to offer you more support and guidance. This book is a great start to a stress-free family, however, some moms may want to go deeper and have a more thorough understanding. In the Stress-free Family System Home Learning Version, I bring the 5 Pillars to life in video format. I go into much greater detail and provide you with the templates, worksheets, and cheat sheets.

Plus, I model Rolling Out Your Routines and the entire Revolutionize Meeting from beginning to end. As a bonus, I also give you word-for-word, complete scripts for everything you need. In the program, there are many real-world examples, too. If you're committed to taking the next step in creating your Stress-Free Family, go to www.theStressfreefamily.com/go. And if you want help with consistency and accountability, there is also an option for ongoing support in implementation and execution, Enjoy your Stress-free Family!

And remember, we're all in this parenting thing together!

Made in the USA
Las Vegas, NV
30 July 2021

27297094R00116